D1070225

Nobody ever said AIDS:

Poems and stories from southern Africa

Compiled and edited by Nobantu Rasebotsa,
Meg Samuelson and Kylie Thomas

KWELA BOOKS

This book is a project of the AIDS and Society Research Unit at the University of Cape Town. It was made possible by generous funding from the Swedish International Development Cooperation Agency (SIDA).

The cover image is reproduced with kind permission of the artist.
"Lien Botha's image of red gloves against a stark white background gives a feeling of cold, bloody isolation. The gloves in *Book of Gloves: The Obstetrician* act as a metaphor of concealment, something used to hide one's identity. An obstetrician's actual rubber gloves are often bloodied in the course of providing medical services, giving life. With such a large, and growing, number of babies born to HIV positive mothers in South Africa, the gloves are also a symbol of bringing into the world new Aids patients." – Kyle D. Kauffman and Marilyn Martin, *AidsArt/South Africa – the visual expression of a pandemic*, catalogue essay, *AIDSART/SOUTH AFRICA.* Iziko: South African National Gallery, Nov 2003 – February 2004.

Cover image by Lien Botha
Cover design by Alexander Kononov
Typography by Nazli Jacobs
Set in Simoncini Garamond
Printed and bound by Paarl Print,
Oosterland Street, Paarl, South Africa

First edition, first printing 2004
ISBN 0-7957-0184-5

http://www.kwela.com

Contents

Foreword

The writers and poets whose works are featured here offer us intimate visions of what it is to live in southern Africa in the time of AIDS. It is not an easy book to read because it is filled with pain, with sorrow and with loss. But this is also why this is such an important book. The intimate ways in which people across all communities are being affected by HIV/AIDS are all too often lost in media reports and statistics. It is creative responses such as these that remind us of the power of art in foregrounding the human face of suffering.

Judge Edwin Cameron, a leading figure in South Africa in the struggle for the rights of people living with HIV/AIDS, has written, "We risk a failure of words, of concepts, of sympathetic insight in the face of AIDS. We need to fight this failure. We need to respond with imagination and compassion to what is happening around us."[1] *Nobody Ever Said AIDS* signals that writers in southern Africa have indeed begun to forge new and imaginative responses to the pandemic. Their words open the space for us as readers to understand, to mourn, and to grieve for the collective losses facing us in southern Africa today. The power of this collection lies in helping to ensure that we will not have remained silent in the face of such enormous loss. In allowing us access to the social and interior worlds of their characters, these writers encourage us to empathise with them and to seek new ways of responding to the pandemic and its devastating effects.

The anthology brings together the voices of many of the region's well-known writers. Many of the writers included in this collection, however, have never been published before, and submitted their work as part of the creative writing competition the editors ran to generate new writing responding to HIV/AIDS. In this sense, this anthology is a book of hope and, in a time of too many sad endings, a book of new beginnings.

As the judge of the short-story competition, I was profoundly moved by the stories I read. Together with Ingrid de Kok, the judge of the poetry competition, I would like to congratulate the competition winners and to encourage all those who sent in their work to continue to seek the words to respond to HIV/AIDS.

NJABULO S. NDEBELE

---

1 Edwin Cameron, "Human Rights, Racism and AIDS: The New Discrimination", *South African Journal on Human Rights* Volume 9, 1993, pg. 29.

Introduction: "Crossing from Solitude"

The poems and stories collected here reflect the reality of living and dying in southern Africa today, where the majority of those who require life-prolonging anti-retroviral therapy do not have access to treatment.[1] This is a book of mourning, a book of despair. But, as Njabulo S. Ndebele writes in the foreword, it is also a book of hope. This collection signifies the emergence of a new body of writing in southern Africa, one that is beginning not only to reflect on HIV/AIDS but also to signal a movement away from silence, stigma and pain, a "crossing from solitude", to quote from Rustum Kozain's poem in this volume. Art allows us to enter into the worlds of others and sometimes even to recognise ourselves in those worlds. The power of words to transport us from isolation to a sense of community, even if only imaginary, is particularly important in a context where so many people are made to feel cast out – alone with illness, with loss, with grief.

When we began this project at the beginning of 2002, there was virtually no published creative writing in southern Africa in English by or about people living with HIV/AIDS, nor by or about those who are witness to their lives and deaths.[2] Addressing this gap has been the motivating force behind the anthology. What does it mean to live in a society where so many young people are dying? How has HIV/AIDS affected the ways in which we live and love and express our desires? How has the pandemic changed our understanding of the world we inhabit and the possible selves we can be within it? We felt that literature would offer rich and imaginative interpretations of, and multiple answers to, these questions.

We decided to run a competition to generate new writing and to encourage previously unpublished writers to reflect on the effects of HIV/AIDS. We invited Njabulo S. Ndebele to judge the short fiction section and Ingrid de Kok to judge the poetry. At the same time we approached well-known writers in the region to respond to the pandemic. The overwhelming response we received is perhaps unsurprising, given the enormous impact of HIV/AIDS on all aspects of life in this region. We would like to thank all those who submitted their writing to us and to congratulate the competition winners: JJ Eli, Khaya Gqibitole and Leila Hall in the short fiction category and Joseph Nhlapo, Nasabanji E. Phiri and Mbonisi Zikhali in the poetry category.

Many of the poems and stories included here protest against the regime of silence that continues to haunt the lives and deaths of southern Africans in the time of AIDS. The title of the anthology, taken from the poem which opens the volume, Eddie Vulani Maluleke's "Nobody Ever Said AIDS", draws attention to one of the most deadly aspects of HIV/AIDS in our societies. Denial runs through all social strata across the region, and perhaps most infamously in South Africa, where the numbers of people who are living with HIV and dying of AIDS, the causal link between HIV and AIDS and even the existence of the pandemic itself have been insistently contested. One of the terrible consequences of this state of denial is the erasure of the lived experiences of people infected and affected by HIV/AIDS.

The difficulty of disclosing one's HIV-positive status in this context is brought to the fore in Norah Mumba's "The Fire Next Time". Although the central character shares her most intimate thoughts with her cousin and confidante, she is unable to tell her she is living with HIV/AIDS. In a similar way Khaya Gqibitole's "Fresh Scars" casts light both on the difficulty of giving voice to what has been made unspeakable, and the crucial role of the listener if testimony is to become possible. The enormity of the tasks of bearing witness to suffering and of facing loss preoccupies many of the writers in this volume. Sindiwe Magona's "Leave-taking" portrays a world in which whole families have been decimated by AIDS and where ceaseless suffering and loss have become too much to bear. In "Milk Blue", Ashraf Jamal explores the ways in which art can bear witness to love and loss that has been rendered publicly ungrievable. His story is inspired by two artworks by Cuban-American artist Felix Gonzalez-Torres, who died of AIDS in 1996. The central character in Jamal's story enacts his own "crossing from solitude" by re-presenting his loss to others in the form of public art memorials.

Aside from Jamal's narrative, and in contrast to most collections of creative writing on HIV/AIDS from North America and Europe, overt representations of gay relationships do not occupy a central place here. Relationships between men and women figure prominently, and this reflects the primarily heterosexual transmission of HIV in sub-Saharan Africa. Leila Hall's "Girls in the Rear-view Mirror" explores the relationship between a truck driver and a sex worker in contemporary Mozambique. Her story confounds the stereotypes that reduce both sex workers and truckers to faceless members of "risk-groups". In "Mpumi's Assignment", Siphiwo Mahala investigates how constructions of masculinity based on sexual prowess and conquest have now become deadly. Similarly, Vivienne Ndlovu shows that in the era of HIV/AIDS, the appellation "Lady-killer" is murderously literal. The impact of HIV/AIDS on the lives of women and girls in this region emerges strongly in the collection, and although gender was not a determinant in our selection principles, we are pleased to note that more than half of the contributors are women. Jenny Robson and Nomthandazo Zondo's "Baba's Gifts" portrays, through the eyes of a rural woman, the difficulties many women face in negotiating safer sexual practices. Their story, like Irene Phalula's "Kusudzula", interrogates patriarchal cultural practices that place women in positions of extreme vulnerability. These works, like many others included here, show that addressing imbalances of power between men and women and revising gendered identities are crucial in the struggle against HIV/AIDS.

Most of the countries in southern Africa have fought protracted battles against foreign oppression, white rule and post-independence dictatorships. Writers in the region have long applied their art to struggles for freedom. Many of the writers included in this volume rightly perceive HIV/AIDS to be a threat to the rights for which they and their predecessors fought in previous decades. They have returned to the language of struggle to confront both the pandemic and the inadequate response of local governments and the international community. Many of the poems and stories, like Roshila Nair's "Fanon's Land" and Nape 'a Motana's "Arise Afrika, Arise!", represent a call for recognition and resistance.

A number of the contributions by South African writers reflect on the ways in which the end of apartheid and the transition to democracy have been overshadowed by sickness and death. In this book, representations of the complexity of life in post-apartheid South Africa speak to, and often against, the celebratory depictions of South Africa as a new nation and a place of life and opportunity. Kaizer Mabhilidi Nyatsumba writes of the relentless deaths of "those to whom / the future belongs" while Kay Brown's story, "The Harvest", shows the extent to which HIV/AIDS has undermined the hopes and expectations of prosperity in post-apartheid South Africa. "What happened to our dreams to change the heart of rage of this country into one of care?" Antjie Krog asks in "A Visit to the Eastern Cape"; "Have we forgotten so soon what we wanted to be?"

The writing in this collection serves to remind us of what it is we have been working and campaigning for and why it is so important to recognise the ongoing struggle that is HIV/AIDS. It also reminds us of the power of representation to document, and even transform, both the social and the political.

Zimbabwean poet Dambudzo Marechera was one of the first southern African writers to die of AIDS. His poems included in this volume were written during the last year of his life, before his death on 18 August 1987 at the age of 35. While the two poems reproduced here were most likely penned before his diagnosis in early 1987, they offer an uncanny premonition of his approaching death. Marechera was a challenging and innovative novelist, poet and playwright who persistently flouted orthodoxy and demanded of us that we cast a more complex gaze on our world. His untimely death struck an irreparable blow at southern African literary culture and was an early indicator of the swathe that AIDS would cut through all aspects of life in the region. We include his poems here in order to honour his memory and because he reminds us of the enduring power of the written word. As Robert Muponde wrote after Marechera's death: "I shall not attend your funeral which is but a mockery. I know you are living."[3]

At the time of Marechera's death, anti-retroviral therapy did not yet exist and there were no active social movements campaigning for the rights of people living with HIV/AIDS in sub-Saharan Africa. The shift in the ways HIV/AIDS has been represented in this region is intimately connected to the existence and increasing visibility of social movements like the Treatment Action Campaign in South Africa. Mthuthuzeli Isaac Skosana's poem, "When I Rise", with which we close this anthology, emerges from this context and was written to express his belief that "there is always life for a person living with HIV/AIDS." The poem conveys a sense of transcendence over suffering, and is also a call for protest against those who deny the impact of HIV/AIDS in southern Africa. It is our hope that the stories and poems in this book will inspire others to rise up and with their words create bridges across the silence of HIV/AIDS.

We would like to thank the Swedish International Development Cooperation Agency for funding this project; the AIDS and Society Research Unit at the University of Cape Town for administering the funds and coordinating the judging of the competition; Jonathan Morgan for suggesting that we run a competition; Viki Elliot for administrative assistance; Lien Botha for granting us permission to use her image on the cover and Annari van der Merwe, Henrietta Rose-Innes and James Woodhouse of Kwela Books. Dozens of friends and colleagues assisted us in distributing our calls for submissions at a range of institutions across the region. They are too many to name here but we thank them collectively for their help and support.

As judges of the competition, Ingrid de Kok and Njabulo S. Ndebele gave generously of their time, and we thank them for helping us to realise our aim of encouraging a new generation of writers in southern Africa.

We also thank the writers for joining us in donating the royalties from this anthology towards distribution of the volume to schools and libraries across southern Africa. This fund is to be administered by the AIDS and Society Research Unit at the University of Cape Town, and for this we thank them in advance. Kylie and Meg thank Dorothy Driver and Kathy Sandler for reading and commenting on our introduction, and Louise Green for her support, patience and letter-writing skills. Kylie also thanks Sandy Chaitowitz and Sasha Rubin, and Meg thanks Brenda Cooper for much-needed advice.

Most of all, we thank all those who sent us their writing.

KYLIE THOMAS AND MEG SAMUELSON
3 MARCH 2004

1 There are approximately 40 million people living with HIV/AIDS across the world. An estimated 26,6 million people live with HIV/AIDS in sub-Saharan Africa; of these, nearly half are in southern Africa. Thus, although southern Africa is home to less than 2% of the world's population, an estimated 30% of all people living with HIV/AIDS can be found in this region. At present, less than 1% of HIV-positive southern Africans have access to anti-retroviral therapy. The figures cited here are from the UNAIDS Sub-Saharan Africa Epidemiological fact sheet (www.unaids.org). On the 19th November 2003 the South African government announced the adoption and details of the operational plan for comprehensive treatment and care for HIV/AIDS. The plan incorporates the provision of anti-retroviral therapy for South Africans living with HIV/AIDS with a CD4 cell count under 200. While the plan certainly signifies a long-awaited shift in government policy, its implementation is still surrounded by controversy, and the majority of South Africans living with HIV/AIDS still await treatment.

2 Some notable exceptions include: the title story in Alexander Kanengoni's *Effortless Tears* (Baobab, 1993); Sindiwe Magona's "A State of Outrage" in *Opening Spaces: An Anthology of Contemporary African Women's Writing* (ed. Yvonne Vera, Heinemann and Baobab: 1999); Kgafela oa Magogodi's *Thy Condom Come: Untamed Love Lines* (New Leaf, 2000); Patrice Matchaba's *Deadly Profit* (David Philip Publishers, 2000); Unity Dow's *Far and Beyon'* (Spinifex Press, 2001); Phaswane Mpe's *Welcome to Our Hillbrow* (University of Natal Press, 2001); J. M. Coetzee's "The Humanities in Africa" (2001; included in *Elizabeth Costello* [Secker & Warburg, 2003]).

3 Robert Muponde, "On Hearing of Marechera's Fall" in Flora Veit-Wild, *Dambudzo Marechera: A Source Book on his Life and Work* (Harare: University of Zimbabwe Publications; London, Melbourne, Munich, New York: Hans Zell, 1992), p. 389.

15

Eddie Vulani Maluleke

Nobody Ever Said AIDS

Oooh
1994
Friday night shebeen
Sis Thandeka's kitchen
Singing loud and rich
To anyone who clapped

The men would sit around
Black Label in one hand
Tapping to the music
Occasionally
Climaxing in a dance
That was me

My heartbeat in the township
My shebeen
In my kitchen
Making people laugh
Making them get up on the floor
And swing their black hips about
No kaffirs there
Just proud black men
That was me

There were the girls
In rouge red glossy lips
Tight red dresses
Waiting for Jimmy
Petros
Jabu
To buy us a drink
That was me
Then

When we knew
That fear came from
A Boer face
Police raids
Rubber bullets
Before
Fear was making love
That was me

Jimmy
Petros
And Jabu
All got sick
And skinny like broomsticks
They started coughing
And couldn't dance any more
They held up their pants
With belts
And just drank and drank
Then they died of TB
In 1996.
TB?
Strong healthy men
Who worked in Jozi
And danced every Friday night
In Sis Thandeka's heartbeat

Other men died too
Men in big cars
Living in Cape Town
America
Britain
France
Healthy men died of
Pneumonia, Flu, Cancer,
TB?
Then the girls in their rouge red glossy lips
Died too
Painfully so,
With hollow eyes

And black spots on their faces
Shebeen queens died
The Boers died
The policemen died
The children were born dying
With black spots on their faces
Freddie Mercury died
Gay men died
Miners died
After they kissed the lips of red berries
Nobody wanted to touch any more
Whether black, white, Indian or coloured
Nobody was making love
That was them

I was
Making love to a new breed
Of Jimmy
Petros
And Jabu

They died of TB too
Then I started coughing
Skinny as a broomstick
With black spots
My sisters' children
Coughed and died
My brother coughed and died
I was coughing and dying
The enemy was in our bodies
Making us cough and die
Eating us like worms
But some of us
Still made love
Still kissed
And made each other cough and die

She died of TB
That was me
Whispering it at funerals
Because nobody ever said AIDS

We all died
Those who used to tap
With a Black Label in one hand
Those who used to sing
Like superstars
Whether we wore rouge red glossy lips
Whether we wore khaki brown
And beat the kaffirs in the prisons
Whether our faces were covered with soot
From the mines
Even if we were old grannies
With our men living in Jozi
Even if we were just born

We all died
Coughed and died
We died of TB
That was us
Whispering it at funerals
Because nobody ever said AIDS

Leila Hall

Girls in the Rear-view Mirror

It was easy to drive past the Pousada Monte Neve during the day. It was on the very outskirts of town, and from the road you hardly noticed it. The building, though fairly large, looked like just another bar or restaurant, its two petrol pumps the only things visible in the vast, empty space around it. By night, however, something about it caught your eye, and you couldn't help but turn your head to look. Huge machines, with bodies of steel and up to eighteen large rubber tyres, hauling trailers, bearing the emblems and goods from manufacturers all over Mozambique and the countries that bordered it.

From the moment the sun began to set, the truckers from the road started to arrive, one after the other, parking their enormous vehicles for the night. It was a regular stop for most of them, somewhere to eat, to rest, to fix any mechanical problems and, for many, after a long, exhausting day on the road, simply a place for a little enjoyment. Soon after the first truckers had arrived, other people began to appear. They would come in groups, their high-heeled boots kicking up the soil in the dusty car park as they wove their way between the trucks, talking graciously to the drivers and flicking their long extensions out of their eyes as they batted their lashes at them. And before long, they were climbing into the trucks with the men, or leading them into the inn, past the bar and restaurant, and up the stairs into the rooms. After a while, they would climb down from the trucks, or they would emerge from the building, with money clutched in their hands as they straightened their short dresses and moved on.

It had long grown dark by the time Luis Pereira parked his truck alongside the others. He had deep brown eyes and a large, solemn mouth surrounded by rough stubble, the result of days on end spent on the road without shaving. Joaquim, his nineteen-year-old nephew, climbed out after him, his hands in his pockets, his eyes wide. Luis looked up at the veranda of the inn. He could see several girls from where he was standing, laughing with a few men or dancing to the loud music coming from the building. He hesitated for a moment, watching them dance, but then turned his back to them and started off in the other direction, making his way between the other trucks until he found where Cael was parked. The smoke rising from behind the trailer told him that something was cooking and he felt his stomach lurch with hunger. He glanced behind his shoulder at Joaquim, slowly trailing behind him.

"Would you fucking hurry up?" he yelled.

Joaquim scowled, but quickened his steps, kicking hard at the dust as he did so. Not for the first time, Luis found himself wishing that he had a son of his own to help him out, not his brother's useless kid. Every time they came here he acted like he'd never seen the place before.

Matias, Jorge and Cael were sitting together between their trucks. Cael's small cooker was burning and maize meal was bubbling inside the pot. The three of them looked up as Luis and Joaquim joined them.

"Oh, you made it," said Cael, turning back to his pot. "What took you so long? You said we'd stay together and then you just fell back . . ."

"We stopped along the way. Sorry." Luis slumped down heavily next to Matias and took out a cigarette. As he lit up, he turned his head again and looked up at the inn. He was looking for Jotinha before he even realised he was doing it, his eyes taking in the dresses and the hair of the girls, searching for anything familiar, any sign of her. He hadn't seen her for over a year now, and he'd almost given up hope of ever seeing her again, but he kept on looking anyway. Just in case. Matias followed his eyes, and also looked up at the building.

"Jotinha's back, by the way." He said it calmly, indifferently.

Luis spun around. "You saw her?"

Matias shook his head. "Gina told us."

"Matias, don't joke with me . . ."

"I'm just telling you what Gina said when she came here!"

"Yeah well, knowing Gina . . ."

He looked away from the inn as he blew out a long trail of smoke, and tried to listen to something Cael was telling the others. But it was impossible to keep his thoughts from wandering. He stood up, throwing his cigarette onto the tarmac and putting it out with his foot. Jorge looked up at him.

"Where you going?"

"Ah . . . just for a beer."

Matias was triumphant. "So you believe me then?"

He didn't answer, simply turned around and walked away. The voices of the others followed him.

"He believes you."

"He's going to look for Jotinha."

He passed a few girls as he walked, but she wasn't among them. He went inside, sat down at the bar and ordered a beer. There weren't many people inside. A truck driver he didn't know had his arms wrapped around a girl a few metres away from where he was sitting. The girl was swaying with the man, one hand around his neck and a can of beer clutched in the other. There were three other people sitting at the bar and a group of girls in a corner of the room, arguing furiously. Otherwise the place was empty. He turned back to the bar, pushing down the sharp pang of disappointment that was rising in his chest. She wasn't there. She was gone for good, and he couldn't bring himself to face it.

He had first come to the Pousada Monte Neve nearly five years before. He had just turned thirty, and it was his first time in a truck, helping out a much older man, Filipe, who regularly stopped here on his journeys down the coast to Maputo. Encouraged by Filipe and some of the other drivers, he had had a few drinks and then, like all the other men around him, he had begun to look at the prostitutes. Some of them looked fierce, like men, with wide cheekbones and stout legs sticking out from underneath their short skirts. Others were more elegant, walking around easily in their high heels, and flirting with the men, enticing them as they wrapped their arms around their necks or their waists, laughing loudly in their ears. He remembered how they had completely bewildered him, almost scared him. And he remembered the first time he had seen her.

Filipe had already disappeared into the inn with a girl on his arm, and he'd been left alone, leaning against his truck with his hands in his pockets, much like Joaquim did nowadays. She was sitting on a concrete bench to the right of the truck, with two other girls. The other two were loud, shouting to the truck drivers with beers in their hands, slightly drunk. She was sitting quietly between them and looked completely out of place. As if she wasn't meant to be there at all. The minute he set eyes on her, something inexplicable had gripped him. No one else seemed to be noticing her at all, but he couldn't bring himself to look away. She had a thoughtful, serious expression, and her eyes were gazing into the distance, so that you got the impression she was thousands of miles away. She had amazing eyes – dark brown, almost black, and shaped like almonds, with incredibly refined lines, as if a sharp pencil had carefully drawn them into her smooth brown skin. The girl on her left, her bubbly laughter ringing into the night, leaned over and whispered something into her ear. And she smiled. It was a small, secret smile and for a minute her dark eyes twinkled. But it was soon gone, like a passing shadow.

When the voice of reason in the back of his head finally spoke, it was hard to listen to anything it said. And yet it managed to bring him back to his senses. He reminded himself that he had a wife and three daughters back in his village. But he'd already been away for nearly two weeks, journeying from his village on the very northern tip of Mozambique down to Maputo, and it would be at least another two before he got back. And all around him there were other men, most of them had wives too, enjoying themselves in the back seats of their trucks or in a room in the inn. It was just sex, he told himself, just sex. And he was a man, with a man's needs. For two weeks, the only other voices he'd heard were Filipe's and the other truck drivers' they happened to meet along the way. Nothing but men. Men's voices, men's company, men's laughter, men's jokes. He was a man, and any normal man needed women, damn it. His mind made up, he took his hands out of his pockets and went over to the bench.

The girl on the right stood up and took his arm, pouting her lips at him.

"You want a girl, lover boy?" she cooed in a sugary voice.

He nodded, his heart beating rapidly.

"Well which one of us do you want?"

"That one over there." His voice was hoarse as he pointed at Jotinha. He hastily cleared his throat. The girl on his arm laughed.

"Jotinha," she let go of him as she sat back down, "you've got a request . . ."

Their eyes met. Her gaze hardened. Everything about her seemed to close up. She stood up and walked with him back to the truck. He could still hear her friends shouting and laughing as he opened the door and let her climb in. She was wearing high-heeled boots and slipped on the metal steps. He caught her and helped her up, but the minute she was inside she shook his hands off her. He felt strangely nervous as he closed the door behind him. He was aware of how strongly the inside of the truck smelt of cigarette smoke and, stupidly, he found himself hoping that she didn't mind. He moved in closer to where she was sitting, but when he felt for her hand her body became so rigid she seemed to freeze in her seat. Her fingers were as small and delicate as the rest of her body. He lifted her face and tried to kiss her but she moved her head away. Her other hand was fumbling, and a minute later she put a condom into his.

"Just get on with it."

He ran his fingers over the plastic covering of the condom, trying to imagine himself with it on. He'd never used one before, and he didn't want to start now. Filipe had told him all about them even before they had left. He said it felt like you were in a plastic bag. He put it down on the seat and cleared his throat.

"Do you charge more without one?"

"Double," she whispered.

"Okay." He felt ready to pay anything.

She lay down. He took off his shirt and lay on top of her. She was warm, her bare skin soft. She turned her head to one side and didn't move. His whole body had already seized up with excitement and yet he felt he wanted more. He wished the whole thing wasn't so rough, if only she could enjoy it too. He could tell only too well that she didn't. Her eyes were closed, her lips pressed so tightly together it looked like she didn't have any. He was already covered in sweat. Her skin was dry against his as he leaned forward and tried to kiss her again. She pulled away. He lay still for a moment, breathing heavily. He gently took hold of her chin and turned her face so that she was facing him. The action seemed to surprise her. She opened her eyes and looked up at him, frowning slightly. For a few minutes she didn't say anything, just stared at his face. He saw something return to her eyes. His breathing gradually slowed down. He leaned forward again and kissed her on the mouth. She didn't pull away. For the first time, he began to feel her heart beat. She opened her mouth to him and began kissing him back. Her arms wrapped themselves around his neck, pulling him in even closer, clinging to him as if she never wanted to let go. He moved his hands slowly up and down her waist and soon they both began to breathe heavily.

They fell asleep with their arms around each other. He couldn't remember ever feeling happier, so at peace with the world. The slamming of the truck door woke him up the following morning. Pale sunlight was streaming in through the small gap in the curtains. The sun was just coming up. The car park was deserted: the girls all gone and the drivers asleep. Everything was quiet against the orange sky, the truck windows gleaming in the light. And Jotinha running towards the inn, her flowered dress flying behind her.

Luis finished his beer and shouted for another. His face had grown hard, bitter, as the memory of that night came flooding back to him. After that, he had stopped at the Pousada Monte Neve on every journey. On his way inland, and on his way back to the coast. For four years, on every journey he made, he saw Jotinha. She soon stopped charging him for their nights together. Once, as they lay together in the dark, he asked her why she had kissed him back that first night.

"No man ever looked at me that way," she replied, her voice trembling, "No man ever even looked me straight in the eye."

It was at that time that he started to worry about her. Each time he saw her she was thinner than ever, she'd taken to coughing and complained of stomach cramps, headaches and diarrhoea. A year ago, he had stopped at the Pousada Monte Neve as usual, and she was gone. He had looked everywhere: the car park, the bar, he'd knocked on all the doors of the rooms upstairs, but he hadn't found her. Maincha was her best friend: stout, loud and a bit rough. She and Jotinha were about as different from each other as you could get, and yet they were like sisters. But even she didn't know where Jotinha had gone or where she had come from, who her family was, or why she had ended up at the Pousada Monte Neve in the first place.

He called to the barman for his third beer. He wanted to drink and drink until her face disappeared from his mind. He looked around as he waited. More truckers had come inside, and the girls had followed them in. His eyes moved quickly from one girl to another almost by habit. And then his breath caught so sharply in his chest that he almost choked. Because suddenly she was there, like a ghost, standing in the corner of the room at the foot of the stairs, wrapped in a thin blanket with Maincha's arm around her shoulders. A girl came up to them with a glass of water, and Maincha gently tried to make Jotinha drink. He was so relieved to see her that he didn't realise anything was wrong. He stumbled to his feet and made his way to the stairs. Maincha opened her mouth slightly and shot a wary glance at the other girl.

"Jotinha." It came out like a gasp, like a breath of fresh air.

He watched as her body stiffened at the sound of his voice. She turned around slowly, and shock went through him like a knife. She looked terrible. She was thinner than he'd ever seen her before, the blanket unable to hide her bony shoulders and thin arms, the long dress she wore was so baggy he was sure it was going to fall off her. Her cheekbones stood out and her skin was no longer smooth and golden brown, but pale and full of blotches and sores. But it was her eyes that pierced his heart. They had always been hard eyes, eyes that had seen too much, and yet in spite of everything were always filled with unmistakable pride. But now they were blank and weak. She slowly lifted her arm. His heart thumped against his chest as her cold hand rested on his cheek, as her thin fingers felt his jaw line. And yet he just stood there, staring down at her, feeling as if she was out of reach. She was like a dream. A dream that had gone wrong. Instead of running to him and throwing her arms around him like he'd imagined, she was just standing there, all her beauty lost. He felt like a man who had been walking in a desert for a year, a man who in that time had never stopped searching for an oasis, and when he'd finally come across one it was only to find that it had dried up.

Maincha went up to Jotinha and whispered something into her ear and then Jotinha turned to Luis with a scared look. Maincha sighed and glanced up at the other girl, who shrugged helplessly. Luis felt frustrated and wanted to ask what it was Jotinha wanted to say, but when he looked at her she didn't say anything, simply gave him a final look and turned away. Maincha wrapped her arm around Jotinha, and he watched them make their way up the stairs. Before he knew it, they were gone. Not a word had passed between them. He could still feel her hand on his cheek.

He wanted to follow them, wanted to put his arms around her, ask her what was wrong, why she was so sick, where she'd been for the past year. He wanted to find out what it was they had been whispering about, what it was Maincha wanted her to say. But he couldn't move. He was so rigid with shock that he didn't know how he managed to get back to the bar. And then anger swept over him, waking him from his trance. Anger at everything, the world, himself, at whoever it was that had destroyed her incredible eyes. His hand shook violently as he lit another cigarette. And then he drank. He downed a beer in a few seconds and yelled for another one. An hour passed. His chest was heavy but something in the pit of his stomach was getting warmer, and his head lighter, with every can. By the time Jorge and Cael appeared at his side, their voices were nothing but distant echoes.

"Oh god . . ."

"He's fucked."

"Luis, what happened?"

"Maybe she *is* back."

"Well, if she was back do you think he would be like this? Huh? Of course she's not back. Gina was just bullshitting us, as usual."

A group of girls shrieked with laughter as Jorge and Cael helped him up and pushed him away from the bar, out into the night. The cold air roused him slightly. He struggled until Jorge and Cael had let go of him, and then told them to piss off. They snapped back at him, but turned around, leaving him alone. He passed another group of girls as he stumbled across the car park. His eyes fell on one of them. He didn't know who it was, and he didn't care. He grabbed her by the shoulders.

"You, come with me." His words were slurred, his voice out of control. The girl immediately backed away, trying to free herself.

"I SAID COME!" he yelled.

She stood her ground firmly and held out her hand. He made a series of growling sounds as he fumbled in the pockets of his jeans. He pulled out everything he had, and dumped it into her palm. Her eyes opened wide. She didn't say anything, just handed it to another girl behind her. Her friend took the money, and tried slipping a condom into her hand, but the girl just shook her head, signalling at Luis with her eyes. She followed him back to the truck. Joaquim was already asleep in the front seat, curled up with his chin resting on his knees. He woke up as Luis climbed in.

"Get out." Luis pushed him roughly. Joaquim, still half-asleep, looked up at him bewildered. Then he saw the girl and understood, and slowly got to his feet.

"I SAID GET OUT!" Luis yelled.

Joaquim scowled and the slam of the truck door closed him out. He didn't look around, just walked away until he found a patch of grass, and lay down on it.

Luis didn't take long with the girl. She climbed out after barely half an hour. He could have asked for more, he could have slapped her if she had refused. But he didn't. He just let her go, and it made him feel even weaker, even more helpless. He fell asleep alone on the back seat.

He was woken later by a noise that pierced straight through his cloudy head, and for a while he just lay in the dark, wondering what it was. Then he realised that someone was standing outside the truck window. He yelled at them to fuck off. It had happened to him before. If you didn't want a girl one night they would make a game out of punishing you, either by banging on your window while you were asleep, or by emptying your tyres so that in the morning you lost half your day trying to pump them up or replace them if the rubber had been torn by a piece of glass from a broken bottle. The noise didn't stop and he realised that someone was calling his name. He climbed into the front, unlocked the door and pushed it open. A girl stood there, holding a torch that shone straight into his eyes. He shielded his face and told her to fuck off again.

"Jotinha wants to see you."

"Huh?"

"Jotinha wants to talk to you."

The voice was small. It was a young girl.

"Where is she?"

"Upstairs in a room."

He looked outside, past the girl. The only lights coming from the inn were in the windows of some of the rooms. He imagined going into a room to see her now. The memory of how sick she had looked was clear in his mind.

"Go away. I don't want to see her. Tell her you couldn't find me."

"She said it was very urgent."

"Tell her you couldn't find me."

He slammed the door and watched as the light hovered over the window for a while, then faded away and disappeared altogether. He wanted to go back to sleep but his chest felt even heavier than the night before and the warm feeling in his stomach and lightness in his head were gone. Instead he had a headache so bad he could hardly sit up, and a horribly dry mouth. He climbed out of the truck into the early morning. He could make out Joaquim quite clearly, still asleep on the grass. No one else was awake, the place was as silent as a grave. He looked over at the inn, emerging in the growing light. It looked so ugly. The yellowish walls reflecting the dying moonlight were dirty, the Coca-Cola sign hanging from the roof old and faded, almost pink. His eyes fell on the upstairs windows of the rooms, and his chest tightened so hard that he was sure he couldn't feel any worse. A wave of nausea swept over him. He tried to steady himself, but his head was spinning. Images from the night kept flashing before his eyes. He fell to his knees and threw up violently. He wiped his mouth with his sleeve as he straightened up again. He could cook some maize meal porridge right now. He could have breakfast here, he told himself, he could go up to the rooms and see Jotinha. Gently stroke her thin face, talk softly to her, maybe even bring her something to eat. But instead he yelled to Joaquim to wake up, and then climbed back in the truck. He wasn't strong enough to go through with it again. To see her after so long, looking so sick, so weak, so unlike the girl that he remembered was more than he could handle. He reached for the bottle of water he kept under his seat and drank it all in one go. Joaquim climbed in and kept throwing him wary looks, as if expecting him to explode. He didn't ask any questions as they drove out of the car park, just stared at the baobabs lining the road.

Luis spent the rest of the journey bitterly regretting driving away. He picked up a different girl at each stop over the next few nights, hoping that it would help him to feel better, less alone maybe, but it only made things worse. He had the strange feeling that he was being disloyal, not to his wife, but to Jotinha. After four days on the road they finally reached Maputo, where they unloaded everything and turned around the next morning for the return journey. Then the fact that they had another four long days left before they got back to the Pousada Monte Neve began to weigh down on his heart. He became restless, so impatient to get there that he insisted on driving whole nights, stopping and parking the truck along the road for a few hours' sleep now and again. It was better that way in any case. The nights were much cooler. By midday, it was so hot that even with their shirts off and all the windows open, the sweat trickled down their foreheads and necks until their whole bodies felt sticky with the stuff. He couldn't help but notice how Joaquim was beginning to develop muscles in place of the thin, crouched body he had had when he'd first started a year ago. He hated the fact that he was watching his brother's son become a man, and not his own. It was just another thing that weighed down on his heart, and it came back every time he looked at Joaquim.

Exactly a week after they had left the Pousada Monte Neve they finally arrived, at nearly eleven at night. Joaquim refused to come out of the truck at all. He sat in his seat, finishing the remains of the sandwiches they had bought that afternoon, silently staring out of the window. Luis was glad of it. He left him in there and climbed out, making his way to the inn with hurried footsteps. It was the strangest feeling, the kind of anticipation that he hadn't felt for so long. He'd hurried to see her before, of course. In those four years he'd been as impatient as he was now, every time they stopped here. But then he had been looking forward to her lips and the feeling of her skin under his hands. This was different. He knew there was no way anything like that would happen. Yet he didn't slow down. The longing inside him was now much more simple – he had to make it up to her, talk to her, tell her he'd missed her. And he didn't care how sick or how thin she looked when he said it. He hurried into the inn, barely glancing at the girls outside. He spotted the tall girl who had brought Jotinha the glass of water. He hadn't recognised her that night, but he remembered her now. Her name was Dinisia, she had been one of Filipe's favourites.

"Have you seen Jotinha?" He asked her.

Dinisia hesitated for a moment. She looked up at him warily, and then gave a sigh.

"Come upstairs," she said after a while.

He followed her without a word, up the wooden staircase, his heart beginning to thump. They came to the narrow corridor, with the doors to the rooms on either side of them. He had hardly ever been up here. A night in a room was relatively cheap, but neither he nor Jotinha had been able to afford it. Dinisia pushed open a door and Luis's stomach lurched as he followed her inside and was met by the smell of dried urine. It was a tiny room, with cement walls, and faded curtains draped over the window. There was a bed in one corner and a chair with a small suitcase on it in the other, and that was it. He frowned. The room was empty. A small bundle of blankets lay on one end of the bed, and one of Jotinha's dresses was spread out on the other. It was the flowered one, the one she had been wearing the first time he had met her. He turned to Dinisia. She avoided his eyes.

"Where's Jotinha?"

She was playing games with him. What was the use of taking him to an empty room and then just standing there like an idiot?

She started shaking her head slowly, looking down at the ground.

"Dinisia . . . stop this shit of yours. Where is she? Where the hell is Jotinha?"

"Luis . . ."

He frowned disbelievingly at her, turned to look at the dress, then back at her. He grabbed her by the shoulders and started to shake her.

"Luis, I'm sorry. She passed away four days ago. She died in her sleep."

He let go of Dinisia's shoulders, his hands hanging loosely at his sides for a moment before he brought them up to his face. Four days. *Four days.* He'd been gone for seven. He'd been driving like a maniac from Maputo for nothing. For a dead woman. He looked up at Dinisia.

"She . . . she died *here?*"

Dinisia nodded. He stared around in horror at the tiny, ugly room. All alone. She must have been all alone.

"Why *here?* What about her family? What about Maincha? Is her family even coming to the funeral?"

"Maincha buried her yesterday. She did it alone."

"Why?" He choked it out desperately. "Why did she die?"

Dinisia was silent for a moment. "She had AIDS."

AIDS. AIDS? Pieces of an incomplete, broken puzzle were trying to come together inside his head. Things that Filipe had told him, words and pictures from a small brochure that someone handed him at a truck stop outside Maputo. AIDS. You couldn't cure it. You got it from sex without a condom. And then a picture that for years he had been trying to forget came to him – a man lying on a mattress in the corner of a dark shack, wearing nothing but a baggy white shirt, and skinnier than anything he could have imagined. Every bone stood out, through the skin and through the shirt – his spine, ribs, shoulders and collarbones. There was no flesh, no muscle. His mouth was pink and swollen, his skin full of sores, and his eyes closed tight. Filipe had been looking for somebody who lived there, a man who owed him money. He had been standing right behind Luis and he had leaned forward and said into his ear, "That's what AIDS does to you."

He had been so scared he had left, afraid that he had caught something from that man, simply from being in the same room as him. The same uncertain fear came back to him every time he thought about it. But it was a feeling that he found himself unable to connect to anything about Jotinha. AIDS. He was holding a piece of thread in his mind, trying to tie things together, but he couldn't. It was such a thin thread, and it was slippery under his clumsy fingers, so that every time he thought he had made a knot it came undone . . .

And then the piercing sound of a baby's cry rang through the room. He jumped as if a bullet had hit him. Dinisia was bent over the small bundle of blankets on the bed. He froze as she picked up the baby, as she shook it desperately, impatiently, her face screwed up with frustration. And his heart seemed to stop as she came over, as she handed it to him, and as he took it without even thinking about it. The baby's cries gradually died into small whimpers, and Jotinha's eyes stared up at him from the middle of a round face with soft, dark skin. He stared back, and he knew it, even before Dinisia said it.

"He's yours, Luis."

He didn't say anything, just picked up his son so that he was upright, and then held him close to his chest, with one hand holding the back of the tiny neck as he shut his eyes and furiously fought back the tears. He kissed the top of his head with trembling lips. The baby stopped whimpering. And he stayed like that, his eyes shut so that he was standing in darkness, in a place where the only thing that was real was the warm feeling against his shirt and the tiny baby he was holding.

"Luis . . ."

He hardly heard Dinisia, he'd almost forgotten that she was in the room. He didn't open his eyes. They were closed so tight that the tears had been squeezed out of them. He could feel them running down his cheeks.

"Jotinha wanted you to have him. That's why she came back. That's why she died in this room. She wanted you to have him."

He held on to the baby as he went over to the bed and sat down, awkwardly putting it back where it had been lying before, and feeling stupid as he tried to arrange the blankets with his huge hands. The baby kicked around in the air, it smiled up at him and gurgled happily. He stared down in astonishment, and then laughed, mostly out of pure surprise. He realised how long it had been since he'd heard the sound of his own laughter. The bed creaked as Dinisia sat down next to him. He became conscious of her eyes on his back and straightened up, clearing his throat as he quickly brushed his hands over his eyes.

"Luis, there's something you should know. Jotinha gave birth in a clinic. The doctors took samples of her and her baby's blood."

He stared blankly back at her.

"When they tested the blood it showed that they were both HIV positive."

"What?"

"The baby . . . is going to have AIDS."

Page five of the brochure. A bright red heading at the top of the page. Mother to child transmission. The thread began tying itself into a perfect knot. He tried to undo it, tried picking it with his fingernail, but it was too tight. There was suddenly a whole line of things, a whole network of people connected. The baby holding onto his finger. Jotinha. His wife. Countless memories of faces, dresses, hairstyles of girls along the road. In the space of a few seconds, the seat in the truck besides his was filled with three different people. The first was Joaquim, sitting in his usual crouched position, with his hands resting on his lap and his eyes fixed on the road. The second was the son that he had always wanted, the one who had never been born. He recognised him from his many dreams, sitting up straight, with large muscles and a deep laugh. And then the third was his other son. A young boy wrapped in a thin blanket, with a spine that stuck out all the way down his back, with bony, hunched shoulders, and a look of helplessness in his almond-shaped eyes. Anger was boiling inside Luis. He wanted to grab the brochure and tear it up so that the only things left were shreds of paper that could be scattered into the wind and never seen again. He wanted to hold Jotinha, wanted her to be light, and pretty and laughing again. He wanted to pick up his healthy baby boy and then he wanted to run away. More than anything he wanted to run, so fast and so far that he would forget who he was or why he had started running in the first place.

He turned his back to Dinisia, and took the baby's tiny hands from his finger as he stood up.

"Luis . . . ?"

He looked down at her.

"You keep the baby."

"What?"

"Keep the baby. I have a wife and children at home. I can't take him."

"Jotinha wanted you to have him."

"I can't take him. Give him to Maincha if you don't want him."

"Maincha left. She got into some Zimbabwean's truck first thing this morning and they left together."

"Dinisia, please then. Just take him."

"Luis . . ." She was growing as impatient as he was desperate, "I clean

33

kitchens all day. I fuck men all night. I am not going to keep a baby who's not mine."

"Well he's not mine either."

"He's yours."

"How do you know? Jotinha fucked men all night as well. It could be any of theirs."

Dinisia shook her head.

"She didn't have many customers, Luis. You know that."

"Well . . . she had others. You don't know he's mine."

"No I don't. But she did."

"How? How the hell would she know?"

"A woman knows, Luis. We do the maths."

"Dinisia . . ."

She shook her head, and spoke softly this time.

"Luis, take your son. There's no one here for him. Jotinha wasn't even my friend. I'm only doing this as a favour to Maincha. Luis, I'm sorry, I really am. But I've done all that I can."

He kept silent.

She took a deep breath and then said, "Take your boy, Luis, take good care of him. Make his short life a happy one. That was what Jotinha wanted."

He looked the other way.

"She chose you, Luis. That's something. She chose you over Maincha, over her family. She loved you. She must have loved you so much. She came back here with her baby for you. She chose to die at *this* fucking truck stop . . . for you."

He was left standing alone in the middle of the room. It was all becoming clearer. He knew now why Maincha had been whispering so urgently, knew why Jotinha had sent someone down to the car park in the middle of the night for him. He hated himself for having got so drunk, for having slammed the door in the girl's face instead of following her to Jotinha, who had been so sick and desperate, who had come all the way back just for him. And in that moment it finally hit him. She was gone forever. She wasn't coming back, and this time there wasn't any kind of hope. There wasn't a voice that kept reminding him that she had promised she would come back one day. Dinisia had been the one to tell him what he'd always wanted to hear Jotinha say, the one thing that he himself had never had the courage to tell her.

"She loved you. She must have loved you so much."

It brought back a flood of memories. Of early mornings when Filipe

34

woke them up because he wanted to get an early start, and they had to say goodbye. Of the smell of her hair as he held her in his arms and she kissed him on the cheek. Of words desperately trying to form sentences in his head as she swung her arms around his neck. Of the aching feeling of regret that came back every time he watched her getting smaller and smaller in the rear-view mirror and he still hadn't told her that he loved her so much that it actually hurt. He went over to the bed and picked up the dress. He buried his face in the thin material, in her soft, quiet smell, and this time he said it, in a hoarse whisper.

"I love you so much."

Then he made up his mind and picked up his son. The baby looked solemn, silently staring up at him as if he understood everything. Luis crumpled Jotinha's dress up into a ball, stuffed it underneath the thin blanket wrapped around the baby, and left the room. He went down the stairs two at a time. He ran all the way back to the truck, turning around only when he got there to take one last look at the inn. At the faded yellow walls, the corrugated iron roof, at the small windows of the rooms upstairs, at the lights and signs he had looked forward to seeing on every single journey he made. Now he felt nothing but pure hatred. He made a fierce promise never to return.

He climbed back into the truck and handed the baby to Joaquim without a word. He looked terrified as he held it, trying to support the head with one arm, and arrange the blankets with the other.

"You be careful with him," he warned Joaquim, before leaning out of the window and backing out of the car park. He swung the truck around and hit the accelerator as they reached the main road. He felt like he was running away. He glanced at his watch as he drove. It was past midnight.

The baby started crying soon after they left. It began with a whimper that, within minutes, turned into a continuous screaming, a bawling that filled the whole truck.

"I think he's tired." Joaquim said, shaking the baby as Dinisia had.

"So then try putting him to sleep."

"How?"

"I don't know. Sing to him or something."

"I can't sing."

Luis sighed, turned sharply and pulled over beside a giant mango tree. Rugged bush and grass stretched out in the moonlight. He turned off the engine and held out his arms.

"Give him to me."

The baby opened his mouth, took a deep breath and let out one long bawl as Joaquim gratefully handed him to Luis. He tried holding him like he'd done before, against his chest, and the crying was muffled by his shirt for a while, but the baby soon broke free, took another breath and kept crying.

"He might be hungry."

"What food do we have?"

"Maize meal . . ."

"What else?"

"I don't know."

"So then go check, don't just sit there telling me you don't know."

Joaquim nodded, turned around and opened the door. Luis went through their box of supplies in his mind. They had water, maize meal, bread, a few oranges. There wasn't any milk, because it never kept for long. What else did you feed a baby? He tried hard to think, tried to remember what kind of things his wife had prepared for his daughters. Nothing came to mind. It didn't really surprise him. He saw his family for a few days every month at the most. The baby was now crying so furiously it was hard to think. It added to the waves of panic rising in his stomach one after the other. He didn't even know how old the baby was. They could try maize meal, maybe even bread and water, but what if that didn't work? His wife would know what to do, but there was more than a week of journeying left before they got to his village. And then what? It was the first time the thought crossed his mind. What would his wife do when he brought back a son that wasn't hers, told her that he had AIDS, that he was going to die in a few years time? He suddenly realised that, in his frustration, he was shaking the baby so hard that it had stopped crying. Joaquim came back and lifted the cardboard box onto his seat.

"There's only a little bit of maize meal left. We've got about half a loaf of bread though."

A strong, wet smell suddenly wafted up to their noses. He screwed up his face and looked over at Joaquim, who grinned like a little boy in spite of himself.

"It's not funny."

"Sorry."

"We haven't got any nappies." He didn't even know how to change a nappy.

Joaquim shrugged, muttered something, and then went back to looking through the box. Luis kept on shaking the baby absentmindedly. Here they were, two men in a truck, parked by the side of the road, with a baby. He tried to imagine the days of journeying that lay ahead, tried to imagine going back home, tried to picture the look on his wife's face. Then he leaned over and opened his door. Joaquim looked at him, but Luis avoided his eyes. He shut the truck door behind him and leaned against it. It was a clear night, and after a few minutes he got used to the dark. There was a cold wind whistling through the branches of the mango tree above him. The baby's hands clutched at his shirt and the little head rested against his chest. A few years. That was what his son's life was going to be. It was going to end just as it was getting started. A few years of getting sicker and sicker every day. A few years of living in a house with a mother that wasn't yours, a father you saw for a few days every month and three older sisters who would probably never accept you as their brother. Luis realised that nothing made sense. He was married to a woman he didn't love, the only woman he had ever really loved was dead, and now that he finally had a son it was only to be told that in a few years he was going to die.

He walked out into the wind that blew so fiercely it stung his eyes. He pulled the blanket over the baby's head and held him even more tightly. The grass was so long it brushed against his arms as he walked. After a while, he came to a large bush. He stopped walking. The soil under the bush was thin, dusty and full of small rocks and branches. He crouched down and began clearing an area with one hand, the wind blowing the dust through his fingers as he worked. He kissed the baby's forehead and put him down on the soil. The baby began to cry the minute he let go of him, miserably, desperately, stopping only now and again to draw in long shuddering breaths.

Luis looked around as if he was afraid someone would hear. But the only movement was the grass and the bushes in the wind. He reached over and tried to arrange the blankets as best as he could. A piece of yellow material caught his eye. He pulled out Jotinha's dress slowly, held on to it for a while, and then put it down on the grass. He turned his back to it as he took off his shirt and covered the baby with that too, making sure that only the eyes and nose weren't wrapped up in material. And then he stayed there, shivering in his thin vest as he crouched over his son, ignoring the thorny branches brushing against his neck in the windy night. More than anything, he just wanted the baby to fall asleep. He started talking aloud to him as he slowly moved his hands soothingly up and down the tiny shoulders. He told him that it would all be fine. The baby stopped crying and seemed to be listening intently.

For over half an hour, all he did was talk and rub the tiny shoulders. And by the end of it the baby was asleep. He would have leaned over and given him a final kiss, but he was afraid of waking him up. Instead, he stood up, picked up Jotinha's dress, and left. He walked back to the truck without a second glance. His whole body felt numb.

Joaquim didn't say anything as he watched him climb in. His eyes took in the yellow dress, the white vest and the fact that Luis no longer had the baby, but then he turned his head and looked the other way. Luis started the engine, and drove back onto the road. He didn't let go of Jotinha's dress. The same hand held the thin, yellow material and the cold steering wheel. Joaquim's snores soon filled the truck. Luis stared at the empty road and kept driving until exhaustion crept over him. He pulled over at the side of the road, locked both doors, climbed into the back seat, and fell asleep with Jotinha's dress over his shoulders.

Dambudzo Marechera

Which One of You Bastards is Death?

All the fish in Lake Kyle refused
The can of worms you call culture –
Do I in the bush a book and a bitch
Render in grandiose terms the tail and theme?
Or fight to life the death that stutters
The doom a layer of dust settles on my window?
Or the speech that in anorak and stout boots
Hobbles from pub to pub seeking a gnarled silence –
Is love the imperious thrust of loins
And honour the dusty defeat on the enemy's face –
Will you say That's how it was uncured but endured?

Not this! How to give back what I never took;
If so, death is our whole condition; to wake
In release from behind the smoked glass
Mad with the delight of seeing you again!

Not this too! I have seen deep within your eyes the lights
Explode.
I crept in, looking for you.
Row upon row slaughtered pigs hung on hooks
Row upon row garrotted memories hung from spikes –

Is life the Nightmare death has when death is asleep?

Ashraf Jamal

Milk Blue

For Felix Gonzalez-Torres, 1957-1996

The bed, unmade, made for two, is milk white. A seam of dark runs beneath the puffed pillows. The pillows overlap. He thinks of tongues; Ross's tongue. There are hollows at the centre of the pillows. The hollow to the right is deep, the hollow to the left shallow. There, once in the shallow cusp, lay Ross's head, a thing of air in his hand, as light to the touch as the head of a newborn child. The whole of him – of Ross – becomes a thing of air, asleep by day, awake at night, eyes wide, unseeing, sensitive to light. The linen curtains, the colour of larkspur, are always drawn. Light filters through the linen sieve, softens, shades. Milk blue.

His eyes shift away from the uneven line of dark beneath the pillows that no light will wither. He studies the milk white folds tongued with blue. He has never lingered upon this mingling of white and blue before. Then it was Ross, always Ross, the man-child, that held his heart, his eye. But now, now that Ross is gone, now, before him, he sees milk, spilt, blue. He will not say that he sees nothing; that there is nothing before him except an empty bed. *Ross* . . . He unfolds the name, listens as it slips, rolls. *Ross* . . . A lover's sigh. A blown kiss.

He stands at the threshold to their bedroom. Do the sheets stir when he softly utters the name? The windows are shut; he will not circulate the air. What he wants is this stillness, this unchanging vista of milk and blue. What, then, is the stirring he sees? A trick of light on a crumpled sheet? Is it the bed that speaks to him now? Out of milk and blue he wills meaning. If not meaning then comfort. Something. Anything. Never nothing.

He is tired. He will not rest. The bed wills him. He cannot shift from the threshold. If he crosses, enters, he knows that he will do so alone. Ross is no longer there, waiting. Beside the bed he sees the porcelain basin and sponge. He will not empty the water; cannot. He will not puff the pillows, straighten the sheets. He will allow no one into the room, not even himself.

For three and a half months this is what he has studied. He opens the door at a definite time; the time he first returns from the hospital and realises that he cannot re-enter the bedroom. Each day, at 11:20 am he opens the door, lingers. The thin thread of dark beneath the pillows strangely consoles him. The light, shifting, seeds the milk with its blue. He grows accustomed to the vigil, expects the blue will come and go. The sky is not his to command. Sometimes the sheets are bathed in a lemon tinctured with blue, sometimes the blue is tinctured with grey. He does not care for blue-grey. The sheets harden then, become a coruscated place of slate. Then the pillows with their crimped hollows are boulders. He never switches on the electric light. He never ventures beyond the threshold. Everything inside the bedroom is unreachable. His clothes, his reading glasses, the unfinished newspaper, the glass of water, the row of plastic bottles with their safety caps. It is he who opened the bottles, he who administered the dosage. He has his own round of medication. Sometimes he has supped believing he does so for both of them, but the waste he holds at bay has claimed Ross.

He has renewed the medication he takes, renewed the clothes, shoes. He no longer cares to read. What occurs in the world is outside his interest. Friends inquire after his welfare. He shuts them out. The gallery calls. They await his offering for a group exhibition. He has made nothing, thought of nothing. Nothing exists outside the bedroom. Yet he must eat, pay for the medication. If he has given up on life, it does not follow that he means to die. Rather, he stands on a threshold between Ross's world and his own. He cannot separate the two.

His dutiful opening of the door at 11:20 am makes him think of clocks; two clocks, synchronised to the very second. When the gallery calls again he has the answer. He presents two battery-operated circular clocks, side by side like the pillows on the bed. He subtitles the piece *Perfect Lovers*. When he reads the catalogue summary he is momentarily gratified. Someone has understood his longing.

> *What do the two clocks convey besides the time of day? . . . Their side-by-side position assumes the power of gesture; they touch. Their synchronisation envisions their relationship, the unison of love. Their identical forms indicate alike lovers; they are homosexuals.*

What the summary cannot say, cannot know, is the extent to which he now exists outside of the perfected sphere of love. Death, a crooked black thread, has come between him and Ross, has joined then separated them. If the circular clocks stand side by side they will never encircle each other, form a space like an upended eye where the one lives inside the other. The circles are sheer, separate. Their twinning says as much of mockery as it does of longing. If the concept is resolved, easily interpreted, it also invites

41

an ideal, which, now, is no longer admissible. Like the bed which he cannot make his own, the ticking clocks with all their seeming harmony sound a death knell.

On the opening night of the exhibition – he goes because it is his duty; because he is sick of desolation – he discovers that the second hands are fractionally out of synch. He says nothing. Desolation grips him. For that fraction of a second he is flung outward, away. Synchrony becomes bitter, remorselessly false. The disjunct second hands are his and Ross's hands, separate, divided by time. He leaves the gallery gutted. Has no one seen the glitch that separates the second hands, mocks his dream of perfected love? If they do, do they care? And if they do care, then why? What does his sentiment matter? In this day and age when fear – like a false hand, a crooked shadow – splits love's soul, who can truly say that perfection counts? Is the love of a man for another man truly a love founded on likeness? Of course not. No two men are the same. Ross was never his mirror. Their hearts were never one. The false hand is true.

That night, for the first time in three and a half months, he enters the bedroom. In his hand he holds a candle. Streetlight filters through the linen sieve, forms pools of red and gold. He sets the candle beside the bed, kneels. With elbows pressed to the edge of the bed, hands clasped, eyes shut, he prays. If oneness is truly possible it is oneness with God. He murmurs, red and gold pressed to the lids of his eyes. He imagines Ross before him with eyes unseeing, ears deadened, Ross's breath involuntary, a matter of the will, a will that is not Ross's but life's ghost heaving through the supine body.

It is forgiveness for which he asks; forgiveness for the false hand that rings true; forgiveness for the fact that he could not stop time, save Ross; forgiveness for the desolation he feels. He knows that tomorrow he will sleep there in the empty bed. He knows that Ross will expect this of him. But first he will pray. To whom? What? A God he has never cared for? Whom he thinks has never cared for his kind? What is this plague, this thin crooked line, that makes a mockery of harmony? Why will no one heed and say: look! It is not your fault, it is the fault of the false hand! Why does he feel such despair when love dies as love will? Surely Ross is content now? Surely there exists a place more comforting than this place where he kneels? If he is a supplicant it is because he knows now that prayer, like light, needs a filter. Love is the filter. Love gives, takes away. Love is a gift, a reproach, an empty bed . . .

At 11:10 the next morning he readies the tripod and camera, waits. At 11:20 he takes the shot. The light is blue upon a bed of milk. Now, months later, now that he has recorded the scene – a scene he thinks of as a testimony to illness, death, love, loss – now he knows he will live there. He knows he will sleep alone. Will Ross visit him? Will Ross say, you are not alone, I am with you? Is it Ross's words he will hear, Ross's voice, or his own? Is Ross inside of him? Beside him? Is Ross the thing of air that beats within?

Beside the bed there is a photograph. The photograph is taken in a canoe. He is the photographer, the absent one for whom Ross grins, his face flushed. In his powerful hands Ross grips the paddles. The chest is thrust out, the arms thrust down. The water all about is the deepest blue; the sky is the colour of larkspur. He places the photograph in a drawer. He does not care for Ross's grin, his flushed cheeks, the power in those arms and chest that once enfolded him with a delicacy that never ceased to surprise him. Now it is the lightness of the head of a newborn child he cherishes, the neck he gently shifts, the body nothing more than skin and bone. He too will one day become a thing as fine. He too will one day pass through the eye of a needle.

Then, when the day comes, when the false hand will sound its truth, he will be ready, waiting. Who will carry him from the bed where he lies? Will Ross return? Will Ross be there to sweep him up in his arms? Will they pass together through milk and blue? Will Ross be his guide; the one who stills his fear; the one who finally plucks the thin dark thread as faithless as a stranger's hair in their bed? For that is what he imagines death to be; a lure in a moment of weakness, a devil-may-care figuration of lust, as thin, as easily shed as a strand of hair; a trace slight, devastating.

In the early days when Ross never knew commitment, it was this thin dark thread, caught in the folds of their bed that would turn love to hate. Then he'd scream, plead. Why, why am I not enough? Ross, spread out across the bed, would look and look, say nothing. What proof could Ross have wanted? At what point would Ross say, now, now I am wholly yours. When he knew that he was dying? When in the clubs and bathhouses he frequented he finally saw his own ghost? When, walking on the lake's shore, they saw the carp, its eye glaucous, dull, its body pecked through to the bone, a star made of birds' feet traced on the shore. It was he who'd pointed out the scene. He, camera in hand, who'd taken the photograph, struck by the beauty of the pattern made by birds' feet. Then it wasn't the beauty of the sand scroll that moved Ross. It was the dead carp gutted to the bone. Was it then, on the lake's shore, that Ross finally turned to him and opened his heart? Love, he knows, can never come too late. Ross needn't have tried to make up for his neglect. It was enough that, in the end, nothing would separate them but the thin dark strand, a strand that now slowly weaves its way towards him.

Before him, on the table, lies the photograph of their bed. He has met with the director of the gallery, made arrangements with a billboard company. Soon the bed of milk and blue will appear in locations throughout the city. The frames of the billboards will be painted the colour of larkspur. If, before, he'd wanted no one to see what he saw, feel the tenderness of his loss, now it is this tenderness, this loss he wants to gift to the world. He wants to part the curtain, say no to darkness.

Paul Schlapobersky

Unclaimed

His place is the low wall on Diagonal Street, in front of the diamond building. The photographers in Joubert Park do better business because they're
near the Noord Street taxi ranks and Park Station, but there's too much
competition over there, and too many dangerous boys. He is busy anyway,
where he sits, and people like the special photos he can do here on the
edge of downtown, with the glass diamond building as a backdrop for
their portraits. For the double exposures he uses old lenses; the ones that
wedding photographers once used to put the bridal couple's faces onto
champagne-bottle labels. First, he takes a photo of the background –
usually the diamond building, or the skyline, but sometimes a Mercedes,
a taxi or a soccer logo sticker – and then he changes lenses and takes the
portrait, without advancing the film, to create the composite image of the
face merging with the background. He also has a lens that allows mirror-
ing of the image. That is a popular one with young men, because they can
have a photo shaking hands with themselves. These are difficult, because
the outstretched hand must be in the right place in the frame to create the
illusion of a man greeting himself.

Mostly, though, his pictures are ordinary portraits; photos to send home
or to give to boyfriends, girlfriends, husbands and wives, or to put on chests
of drawers. Many are documents of the first day on the job; security guards
and police in uniform, office workers in white shirts with ties, women in
matching skirts and tops. People in church outfits or in traditional dress.
The people are from everywhere: Zairians, Togolese, Zambians, Mozam-
bicans and South Africans from all over the country.

His long box of photographs is organised according to the date when
the photo was taken. He tells people they can come back after three days
(except if it rains, because then he can't finish his film and take it to the
Photomat), but some people take a long time to return, and some never
come back. In the box there is space for about six months of photos and
after that he takes them out of the box and leaves them at home.

Over the years the unclaimed photographs have started to take up space
in the tiny bachelor flat that he shares in Berea. The man he lives with is a
Togolese whose unsuppressed eccentricities impress the photographer,

who himself works hard to hide his differences, to fit in as much as possible and draw no attention to himself in this hard city. The Togolese shouts at everyone in French, wears a grey suit while selling vegetables on Rockey Street, and had for a long time a tame white rabbit that sat under his stall every day, eating cabbage leaves in the shade. On the day that a crowd rampaged down the street, overturning the stalls of foreign traders, the rabbit bolted in fear from beneath the table and was killed by a car. That day the Togolese man stood in the middle of the road in his torn suit, and screamed in French at no one and everyone, and when he came home he shouted at the photographer about the amount of space the boxes take up in their small home, before curling up on his mattress, still in his suit.

The photographer is always on the verge of carrying the boxes down to the pavement below for the rubbish trucks to take away, but can never do it. The unclaimed photos are a problem; not exactly precious, but impossible to throw away. Partly, it's because they are his workmanship, but also simply because portraits of strangers, like letters written by hand – even a strange hand – are difficult to put in the rubbish bin. Though he handles hundreds of photographs a week, he still feels strange when he finds someone's picture lying on a sidewalk in the city, as if its presence there is a mistake; as if it must have been lost by accident.

One day, there was a woman who spoke the photographer's distant and rare language and who had many photographs taken in her orange dress. They had both agreed on the red-brick wall of the Reserve Bank for the backdrop of her portraits, after checking out the light at the fountain and beneath the porticos of the shops. She spoke to the photographer of the need to send these portraits home quickly, as a reminder. A reminder of what, he had asked. Had she left home so long ago that nobody would recognise her?

When she had first arrived at his low wall in the sun, it had seemed to the photographer that there was a darkness falling across each of this woman's movements and weaving itself through her clipped sentences; a heaviness and sadness hanging on her thin frame. His delight at recognising the voice of a person from home, and his natural friendliness, brought her out of her shadows momentarily, and they talked for a while of their faraway land. As soon as the photos were taken, however, she seemed to grow tired and she suddenly seemed smaller and frailer than she had a moment before. She left, and repeated his "three days" mechanically before disappearing around the corner.

She never came back for her pictures, and he realised after about a week that every day he was waiting for her to return. It was that woman who never returned whose absence disturbed the heavy silt of fear lining the bottom of him, swirling it through his being – fear of the dark things convulsing the city, of murder and car crashes and AIDS, of the wild and powerful forces that lay just beyond the frames of his innocent and optimistic pictures.

That woman's photographs eventually joined the others in his room, but on the wall next to the stove, not in a box on the floor. He looks at them sometimes, and tries to see something in them that will answer the questions he has for her. Since her, he has been weighed down by a sadness he feels every evening when he opens the door and sees the brown boxes, knowing that before he goes to bed he will have to add to them from his portable work box. He knows there are many reasons why people don't pick up their photos – they forget or run out of money. But he also knows that this city steals many of his customers away, pulling them off its streets indifferently, leaving only their unclaimed pictures.

Karen Press

flakes of the light falling

(plague poem)

approximately and here also
one in four vanishing
even as we speak –

lightly and without technique they are dying
slowly and beyond the duration of love

good citizens of a good country, dying modestly
embrace of the infected is a national project
rejection the prerogative of the intimate circle

metaphors of love crack open,
out of their varnished shells
people emerge, dying

howling is not possible where children sleep
and their mothers, dying blossoms of blue light
inside the cloudbursts of men's love

very close to the ground children and their mothers
and then also their fathers die here
in the way of poor people, struggling
for small dignities and the simplest food
astonished softly over and over
I touch my lips to each death

approximately and here also
one in four vanishing –

how many little pallbearers for one coffin?
to wrap your father in a sheet takes days and days
tangling yourself in the web of bones
who will bury him if you don't?
you saw helplessly at the tree

all night my little clock makes a vastly solemn noise
like a child treading the long dark passage
in her grandfather's shoes

among blades of grass, against crumbled walls
let cows offer their udders to the babies
lying upturned, helpless as beetles

metaphors of love crack open

suddenly one day you will hear
how silently the black sky blazes
how wildly the empty street is searching
for a footstep

we are ending, we are ending
flakes of the light falling away

———

Nosipho Kota

When You Died

For X. Duma, who died of AIDS in December 2000

When you died
the landscape changed
the coffee that I was drinking turned cold
my bath water turned red
the dogs stopped barking
the chickens came home
the children's giggles stopped,
when you died.

Norah Mumba

The Fire Next Time

> For the great day of his wrath is come; and who shall be able to stand?
> Revelations 6:17

> . . . for he is like a refiner's fire . . .
> Malachi 3:2

> God gave Noah the rainbow sign,
> No more water, the fire next time!
> James Baldwin, *The Fire Next Time*

My dearest Zondiwe,
You are right. The first letter I wrote to you when I'd just got here was full of enthusiasm. As you can imagine, I was full of the excitement of a first trip away from home, and so far away at that. Europe is everything that we always imagined it to be when all of us young friends back home sat under the African sun and dreamed about how we would get here some day to study among the Europeans and come to understand their life, their culture, acquire their knowledge. Do you recall how the guys would argue at length about the origins of civilisation, about the relationship between the two continents, how Europe and Africa were like two conflicting spouses, and so on and so forth, while we girls got distracted by the more mundane matters of life like oiling and braiding our hair? Those hot lazy afternoons when we would seek refuge under the big jacaranda tree in your mother's garden, covered by a shower of violet; those afternoons followed by bright moonlit nights so favoured by young lovers.

We did most of our growing up then, for that was the age at which we were able to think life over and make plans for the future. Of course we were not always right about things. Unfortunately youth is also the time in one's life when one is convinced that one knows everything and that the older people and their caution and advice are pedantic bores! Your mother, my mother and everyone else's mothers were simply out to spoil our fun. What did they know about how enlightened we were? How we understood issues so much better than they did because we were in the "flow" while their world was so far removed from ours? How the fathers, when they had time to throw in some support for their wives' tired words, were merely trying to keep the peace.

Then again, one cannot deny the interesting quiet conversations with our mothers when there was no conflict lying on the table to create a vicious divide. Those conversations taught us, nurtured us and gave us a sense of belonging. The saddest state in life must surely be not having had those intimate times with the one whose back was the warmest place in the world, whose breast was the definition of love itself. She whose arms gave you protection and rescued you from the shock of gravity, and who offered succour unfailingly in life's many difficult moments. When she used her tongue in chastisement, you only had to remember how many times she used it in soothing tones when you needed it most, and you allowed her the liberty of a few invectives.

Zondi, ever since I've been out here I have had a lot of time to think. I suppose it's the effect of being alone in a strange land away from home. I miss being with you all, hearing familiar sounds and voices. Even the annoying routines of life become so dear when they are no longer there. Your letters are so precious to me. I hear in them all those sounds and voices that I long for, and they keep me in touch with my circle of family and friends but, above all, I can pretend that you are sitting next to me talking. I hear you, Zondi, in your confident manner firmly asserting: "one fine day . . ." after we have shared those wishes and aspirations about what we will do for ourselves, for our parents and for our children, then wondered how much of it we would be able to achieve. You are a great one for seeing beyond the problems and obstacles of today. I wish I were as forward-looking and as confident of the future as you always are.

Well, Zondi, it's back to my books for now. I need to get that post-graduate degree. That is how I am going to be able to set my eyes on you again very soon, one fine day!

With much love,
Your cousin Thokoza

"Zondi, Zondi . . .," he had to call several times before she broke out of her reverie. Even then she gave him the uninterested look of someone wrenched from more important matters. Zondiwe had taken to re-reading her letters from Thokoza as a substitute compensating for her physical absence. Lately she spent long periods lost in a world of her own which Joe wished he could penetrate. She spent many hours after a working day sitting next to him, and all night lying beside him in their matrimonial bed, yet it was as though she was not really there. She breathed quietly next to him, and he felt the warmth of her body, but the one thing he desired most, her total presence, was out of his reach.

Joe and Zondi had been a close couple. Everyone envied the bond between them, even before they married. It was not a mere routine pronouncement when the priest declared them one from that time forth, for better or for worse. They had gone to the church already one in spirit. It was what many described as a match made in heaven. Even the elements approved – the sun shone brightly on their wedding day during a heavily overcast week in December, a month of relentless tropical rain. Eleven months later the twins were born, arriving into the world screaming their healthy lungs out to the pleasure of their proud parents. Their birth finally thawed the ice between Joe's mother and Zondi. She had been resentful of her son's choice of wife and assumed that Zondi, a professional woman, would not be keen to bear children. Brought up in the old school, Joe's mother valued a married woman by the number of children she bore. This Zondi, who was a successful senior nurse at the big hospital and quickly rising in her profession, was not the sort of woman a mother-in-law could picture carrying one pregnancy after another and sitting at home to nurse the babies. Oh no, she was destined to look after other people's babies at work and, as she warned her son, knew all the modern medicines that stopped women from having babies. But Zondi had proved her wrong by becoming a mother so soon after the wedding. Two at one go, and boys at that, was not bad at all. She danced attendance on her daughter-in-law, much to the amusement of all.

After Joe's mother left reluctantly two months later, Joe and Zondi felt the pressure of the amount of time the two boys demanded. One baby waking up and bellowing would immediately provoke the other so that they needed two pairs of hands in order to cope. Zondi had to double the customary three months maternity leave so that by the time she returned to work, one elderly nanny was able to look after the babies without losing her mind. MaZulu became a pillar of the Ngwenya family. She went about her business with a cheerful attitude, mothering not only the lively twins but also their young, hardworking parents. In no time at all she knew both Joe and Zondi as well as if they were her own son and daughter, and won their total confidence. Zondi was able to relax even if she had to spend long hours at the hospital, knowing the boys were in good hands, and Joe's anxious phone calls home gradually reduced.

Zondi's workload was ordinarily heavy, but the week they had to treat a group of children from a nearby orphanage was particularly hectic. The doctors decided to do a full battery of health tests on the children, particularly the frail-looking ones. As expected, several of them tested HIV positive. There was among them a girl of about three, whose head seemed to weigh more than the rest of her body. She stared at Zondi as she held her up. She had profound eyes which, under better circumstances, should have been filled with laughter. She was obviously in constant pain. When Zondi moved on to the next child, the little girl's eyes followed her as if communicating something. Zondi found herself drawn back.

"What is your name?" she asked her, but got no response from the eyes that remained fastened on her.

"That's Tammy, she doesn't talk much," offered the nun who had accompanied the children. "She seems to like you."

Later at home, Zondi told Joe about little Tammy, not that there was much to tell, save that she had a new friend. She was interrupted by the bellicose cry of one of the twins, quickly followed by the lower wail of his brother.

"There goes Mark, and he has woken Matthew, as always."

Joe, who still had difficulty telling his sons apart, looked admiringly at Zondi as he got up to follow her to the children's bed.

"You get Matthew and I'll take care of Mark in a moment," she said to Joe as she walked past the bed.

Joe stood uncertainly, then picked up the baby nearest to him. Zondi returned to the room and smiled.

"That's Mark, Joe. Don't blush, I just wanted you to confess that you get the boys mixed up."

They laughed together as they tended to the babies, now more than a year old.

The orphans were kept in the ward for three days, while various specialists examined them. Zondi's friendship with Tammy grew. She started to respond to her in one-word answers. Sister Perpetual told Zondi a little more about Tammy, how she had been brought to the orphanage by relatives after both her parents died of AIDS and her grandmother had no means of looking after her. She had older siblings whose fate was unknown.

"Probably among the ranks of Lusaka's swarming numbers of street children," surmised Sister Perpetual.

When the children left, Zondi asked if she could go to the orphanage to visit Tammy. Sister Perpetual encouraged her.

"God knows, she could use some loving such as you have shown her these days that she has been here. We shall be grateful if you remember her, busy as you are, Nurse Ngwenya."

On her first visit to the orphanage, Joe and the twins accompanied her. The nuns were delighted to have them there and Sister Perpetual took them to see Tammy. When they were leaving, Zondi promised she would be back before long.

"Thank you for the fruits and sweets," said the Reverend Mother, seeing them off.

"We weren't sure what was appropriate. Please tell us if there is anything in particular you need," said Zondi.

"Oh, we would rather you give within your means, my dear. Whatever you bring will have a use for the children."

Joe made a mental note to speak to his colleagues at the office so that they could put together a meaningful donation for the orphanage. The visit had really opened his eyes, and he pondered over what he had seen as they drove home.

A circular written by the Chief Medical Officer was passed round the wards, inviting all ranks of medical personnel to avail themselves for voluntary HIV testing. It generated a lot of discussion among both doctors and nurses. People debated at length the pros and cons of subjecting themselves to the test.

"If we, the caregivers, are reluctant to find out our status, what can we expect of laymen?" argued one nurse.

There were some murmurs of agreement, but not from all. Ultimately, it was up to each individual. Zondi was among the few who were quick to rise to the challenge and went to have the test done, even before discussing it with Joe.

He had been so busy lately at the office. A vacancy had opened in the management structure following the retirement of one senior manager, and Joe was on his way up the ladder. He was anxious to prove that he deserved the promotion and so did not decline tasks even when it meant that he was constantly on the move, and often out of town. He counted himself lucky that Zondi was so understanding. She did not complain about having to look after the boys all by herself outside MaZulu's hours. She did not get upset when he overlooked his routine responsibilities. She was only a little ruffled when he did not turn up for a social outing with their long-time friends, Clara and Peter.

"You could have phoned me, Joe, just to warn me. Peter and Clara drove from the other end of town to come and meet us, and you were nowhere to be seen."

Joe had looked appropriately apologetic and proceeded to tell Zondi how much money had been raised at his office towards supporting the orphanage. He knew that it would pacify her.

"Besides, it seems I have to take on even more responsibilities now," said Joe.

"Why is that? Who else is retiring?"

"Not retiring. Our company is having a manpower crisis. People are constantly off sick. So many hours are lost," explained Joe in an irritated tone.

"Oh well, people cannot help being sick. We have a similar problem at the hospital."

"But at least your staff still come to the office since that's where the help is. Our people, on the other hand, spend many valuable hours with you lot."

Zondi laughed despite herself.

Later, over drinks with Clara and Peter at Joe's staff club, they talked about the rising AIDS crisis that was depleting the workforce, filling orphanages and swelling the streets with children. The government was too overwhelmed to be of any help. Not that there had ever been any coherent social security policy from government anyway, asserted Peter sardonically. Clara argued that there was a whole Social Welfare department. A leftover from the colonial government structure, Peter rebutted, which the new government was either too embarrassed to abolish or hoped would collapse with time as the office-holders retired or died and were deliberately not replaced. So, as government smartly abdicated responsibility, families were left creaking under the growing weight of more orphans to be distributed among fewer surviving relatives, who wished they were dead too. Companies paid out colossal sums in funeral grants for their dying workers, while the survivors were constantly out of action due to illness. Churches were active seven days a week conducting funerals for their departed congregation members, while there were fewer offerings on Sundays to sustain the clergy.

"The tragedy is that AIDS is wiping out a whole generation of our most vital, most active age group. We will soon be looking at a future with only the very old and the very young," Joe concluded, to the agreement of all.

When she collected the results of her test, Zondi was dumbfounded. She sat in the nearest chair and looked at the slip of paper again, as if it were not real. The doctor was saying something to her, she did not know what. She gathered herself up and left the office. Instead of returning to her ward, she walked out of the hospital premises and headed for home where

MaZulu was surprised to see her so early. The elderly woman knew instinctively that something was wrong, but she was tactful and did not pry.

Two hours later, Zondi was still asking herself the same questions. How? Why me? Then it hit her that other people apart from her were affected by this "verdict". Oh God, the twins! And Joe . . . Joe, how is it that I turn out to be HIV positive unless . . . Her mind was crowded with so many thoughts. Concentrate on the children, she told herself, concentrate on Mark and Matthew. She walked out of the bedroom and went to where the boys were playing happily with MaZulu.

"You can go home now, have an early evening" she told the elderly woman.

"If you are sure, madam."

"I'm very sure, MaZulu. Go home to your family."

I don't know how much time I have left with mine, she thought.

Joe did not come back until well into the night. Zondi went through the motions of getting him his supper and sat with him as he ate. He talked about his day. He has forgotten to ask me about mine, she thought. A feeling of numbness had overtaken her. When they finally got into bed, she calmly told him:

"I went for an HIV test, Joe."

Silence, then he responded: "Oh."

She waited, and when he did not say anything else she continued, "That was three days ago." She thought she felt him tense up. "I got the results today. Positive."

Joe jerked up into a sitting position. Zondi had her back to him and lay quietly. He slumped down like a deflated balloon emptied of air, reduced to a limp rubber tongue. She waited a few more moments for his fire and, when it was not forthcoming, surrendered herself to numbness.

In the morning, after Joe left, Zondi phoned the hospital intending to give excuses, but the matron insisted that she report to her workstation. When Zondi arrived, the matron was waiting for her and took her into her office.

"Nurse, I won't beat about the bush. I know about your HIV test result."

"I thought that was supposed to be confidential," Zondi started to protest.

"It is, except when my best nurse disappears without reason soon after getting the result, then it has been announced from a hilltop."

Zondi sighed with resignation. Of course the matron was right. Everyone must know by now.

"I am not flattering you when I say you are my best nurse. You are, and

I do not want to lose you, so I am sending you for counselling sessions with the best practitioner I know. You are going to continue being the best regardless of this result. I need you alive, and so does your family."

Her conversation with the matron gave Zondi the impetus to move. She decided to share the news of her status with a few trusted friends at work, and then phoned Clara who came over immediately.

"Zondi, you are the one in the medical field so you have professional knowledge. One thing I do know, though, is that you need to talk to someone old, someone who is in touch with the spirits of our forefathers and our foremothers."

"Clara, you are not going to take me on the rounds of traditional doctors, are you?"

"Certainly not! Tomorrow is your day off, I know, so get ready. I'm coming to get you."

With the boys sleeping and Joe not yet back, Zondi sought solace in re-reading letters from Thokoza in England.

> Your letters are so precious to me. I hear in them all those sounds and voices that I long for, and they keep me in touch with my circle of family and friends but, above all, I can pretend that you are sitting next to me talking. I hear you, Zondi, in your confident manner firmly asserting: "one fine day . . ." after we have shared those wishes and aspirations about what we will do for ourselves, for our parents and for our children, then wondered how much of it we would be able to achieve. You are a great one for seeing beyond the problems and obstacles of today. I wish I were as forward-looking and as confident of the future as you always are.

Yes, the days of our youth were so full of promise, thought Zondi. How were we to know that our lives would be disrupted by this fire raging all over Africa? This fire of as yet unknown origins that has left no family untouched and is determined to destroy each household. Thoko, if only you were here. You would know the right things to say. You give me credit for being forward-looking and confident; I'm afraid that's all gone from me now. I want so much to share with you my terror at what is happening inside my body right now, but I can't.

Instead of writing to her cousin about her fears of what the future held for her children without her, and possibly without their father too, Zondi wrote about the pleasantries of mothering, and complained that Thoko was not writing as often as she used to. That was the closest she came to opening her heart and crying out to her cousin.

> . . . As usual, you have caught me out. I know that I promised I would write every week, but that was before I saw the workload I have to deal with. One good thing, though, is that I do not have to go chasing documents all over the show. The university library is a massive storehouse of just about all the information I need. The books are contemporary editions and journal issues fall off the press onto the library racks. What is not on the shelves is easily accessed with the touch of a few buttons on the computer. Life in these developed countries is without tears. I can't wait to come and revive those philosophical discussions with the guys.
>
> So the twins are keeping you and Joe fully occupied, but that is only to be expected. Whatever you do, don't ever give up your job to stay at home and look after the children. By the time your next child is born (how many more months do you have to go now?) you will be well into that exhausted state from which many housewives sink into lethargy. In case you are thinking how come I'm making myself out to be an authority on the subject, I saw enough of how my mother struggled with eight of us – the poor woman was like a beast of burden. You and I are lucky that we have careers outside the home. You didn't go to college so that you could end up mothering Joe's children as a lifetime vocation . . . Give my love to the family and to all our friends.

The next morning Clara turned up as she had promised and they set off for their mystery destination. Before long Zondi realised that she was being driven to her grandmother's house just outside town. MaJere, as her grandmother was fondly known, liked it here where her son, Zondi's youngest uncle, grew crops and kept chickens for sale. They were surrounded by beautiful natural bush, the closest MaJere could get to being back at the village, she often declared. There were no car horns there, no industrial pollution in the air and no uncultured town people peddling their corrupted wares all over where decent folk needed to walk.

Seeing MaJere lightened Zondi's heart. Even so, the old woman knew something was up. She received them with her usual cheerfulness, made a fuss over them and, after she had them seated on an elaborately woven reed mat, she asked: "What has gone wrong, Zondiwe? Something is not right, your spirit is not singing its usual song today."

Clara gave Zondi a knowing look. Zondi turned to her grandmother and tears started to flow down her cheeks. The old woman clapped her hands loudly to shoo off some chickens that had ventured too close to where her basket lay full of shelled groundnuts.

"Ha, every hen must go to sit on its own eggs. She cannot sit on another hen's eggs and expect peace. How does a hen know what will hatch out of eggs which she did not lay?"

Zondi knew that MaJere was not speaking of hens. They listened attentively as the woman went into a soliloquy.

A little bird flew back from the forest, from the forest to its nest it found its chick fast asleep, its chick fast asleep, the little bird said: wake up, little one. Wake up, little one, let us share some words, share some words for with words come wisdom . . .

Zondi recalled from the deep recesses of her mind a rhyme that her mother, one of MaJere's many daughters, used to sing to her when she was a little child, oh so little, the sound that used to soothe her to sleep. MaJere was half talking, half humming. The tears stopped flowing. In their place came warmth and lightness. Zondi felt herself slowly lifted on the wings of MaJere's words, up and up until she could see the tops of the trees and the ground was one brown carpet spread from one end of the earth to the other. She flew over ridges that were springs and rivers, on towards a place where the earth was no longer brown but all green. She knew in her heart that that was where she wanted to get to but there seemed to be a power beyond herself that kept her from breaking through. She knew she must not give up. As long as there was wind under her wings, she could continue flying, and that is what mattered. The little bird wanted to share with her chick what she had encountered as she flew. The answer was up there somewhere.

As the two friends left MaJere at the end of the day, Zondi took with her an image of her grandmother, her aged face reminiscent of the ridged ground she saw from the air, standing with her back to the setting sun. Zondi had a vision of the legendary phoenix rising from the ashes in a flame of fire.

They drove back in silence, each one lost in her thoughts. Zondi had a sudden longing to visit the orphanage and see Tammy again.

At home, Zondi went through her neat pile of letters and dwelled on the one Thoko wrote shortly after MaJere's last birthday celebration. It was an event the family made a big occasion of because it is not always easy to make time to celebrate the lives of those you love while they are still with you on this earth, and after they are gone, it is too late. Thoko was so sorry not to have been there.

> . . . Yes, Chipo wrote me from Harare. The following day I heard from Dingi in Cape Town. They were both talking about travelling home for MaJere's 80th birthday. What an exciting time it must have been, with all the family there, except me of course. I spent a dejected day wishing I were in the middle of that loving crowd. You did tell her why I couldn't be there, didn't you? One thing is for sure, I'll be there for her 90th birthday! Grandmother is so strong, we should be making plans for her 100th. She is one person who is defying those depressingly low life expectancy figures. Last I heard, it was about thirty-four years for women. To think that young as we are, we are just about getting beyond the country's life expectancy. Between them, poverty and HIV/AIDS are taking a devastating toll on our people . . .

It is strange how one's life can change so completely, thought Zondi. One day she was just a happy wife, mother and professional woman. The next, she was among the millions living under the cloud of HIV/AIDS – "the fire next time", as it has been called. They say that after God punished the world with a flood and saved Noah and his family, he pledged never to use water as punishment again. But take heed, the fire next time!

Is this how prisoners condemned to death felt? Listening to seconds ticking by and wondering which one would be the last?

She sat in on conferences and seminars on HIV/AIDS and heard a lot of words that meant very little to her. It seemed that people the world over had said just about everything there was to be said about this epidemic and the virus, and now everything was mere repetition. Statistics and reports were addressing those whose occupation was the epidemic, while they did nothing to touch individual suffering and pain.

At the end of year 2000, 25 million people in sub-Saharan Africa were estimated to be infected with AIDS, while six to seven thousand were dying daily from it. Year 2002 estimates are that nearly 12 million young people aged between 15 and 24 are infected with HIV/AIDS while 6000 young people acquire the infection daily.

It was like conscripting an army so that you could be rescued from a war and then watching them waste all their ammunition on target practice in the air while you perish in the battle on the ground.

When she went to visit Tammy and the other children at the orphanage, their appreciative smiles and expressions warmed her heart. On her next visit she took along some friends. Together they made a difference in the lives of the children – their informal support group had a therapeutic effect on both the recipients and the caregivers.

Back home, Zondi faced the duty of telling members of her family what was happening to her. As expected, there was a lot of distress and even recriminations. Her mother swore she would never talk to Joe again for as long as she lived. Joe's mother, on the other hand, surprised everyone when she declared she would be there to give the couple all the support they needed. Until now, only Clara and Thokoza far away in England knew that Zondi was pregnant. What Thokoza did not know, however, was the storm surrounding the pregnancy.

> . . . I am sorry to hear about your constant tiredness. It must be the weight of that baby you are carrying. I was going to do some shopping in advance but then you are not sure whether you are carrying a boy or a girl. I am keeping my fingers crossed for a girl, seeing as the twins are boys . . .

Joe was fighting his own ghosts. Lying next to Zondi every night, not exchanging so many words, he had a lot of time to reflect and he did not like what he saw of himself. He wished that he could have handled matters differently. Zondi was the perfect wife. This thing that had come between them could very well have been his fault. He agonised over a couple of indiscretions committed at a time of great stress in his career, and even cast his mind back to the period before he met his wife. Indiscretions that to him were totally meaningless and had been quickly pushed to the back of his mind – some wanton moments of excitement with faceless and nameless women. There would always be only one woman for him – Zondiwe, yet he had not been man enough to sit and talk things over with her. He let her carry the whole load on her shoulders. He had lost her respect, and he knew it. What could he do now to mend fences? Should he go for the test also, to reassure his wife that they were both ill? What comfort was it, for a mother to know that the father of her children was dying alongside her? Zondi had sunk so fast because of the second pregnancy, so maybe he had a little more time. But how much time? And now he wrestled with these ghosts every waking moment.

If only he had said something when I told him, Zondi thought for the umpteenth time, lying next to her husband. Anything. She did not plan it, but she found herself going cold against him. When she had told him she thought she was pregnant, he had suggested that in view of her status she should consider having an abortion. She had ignored him as though he had not spoken. Only the twins kept some string attached between them. Some nights in bed he thought he would try and talk to her, but their strained, polite conversations were devoid of the closeness they had shared before.

The pregnancy took its toll on her. Writing to Thokoza in England she talked of tiredness. She wanted to protect her cousin from the gravity of her situation at all costs. She did not write about the herpes zoster, that excruciatingly painful disorder of the skin ironically referred to as "the fire of God". The scars it left were a constant reminder of her agony, a branding. Small discomforts grew into major conditions because her body's immune system was compromised. Thoko wrote regularly, and her letters were a source of comfort to Zondi. When she was feeling particularly low, she would take them out and read them again. Sometimes she felt a sense of guilt at not telling Thokoza the truth, but she justified it by telling herself it was because her cousin was so far away from home, the truth would only ruin her ability to concentrate on her studies.

> . . . Congratulations! And double celebrations that it is a girl. Every mother needs a daughter in order to gain a sense of having completed the procreation cycle. Tell Joe I am extremely flattered that you two named the little angel after me. God knows, I don't deserve the honour. Please, please send me that snapshot quickly. I want to display it on my desk. Little Thokoza is my good luck charm. You know, you really should ask your mother to stay a little longer with you until that tiredness wears off. Pregnancy is hard on the body . . .

Poor Thokoza, if only she knew what the tiredness was about. In her mind Zondi spoke to Thokoza forthrightly, but her letters continued to conceal the truth. She was feeling so heavy with their deceptive nature that she considered not writing at all, but she knew that would injure her favourite cousin. Oh Thokoza, I wish you would come home soon. I feel my time drawing near. I am going to make that flight to the green expanse yonder where peace awaits me.

Zondi was too tired to get to the phone when Sister Perpetual phoned. MaZulu took the message. Tammy had died that morning. The nuns thought Zondi should know because she was the closest the little girl had to 'next of kin'. Although she thought she had no more room for further pain, Zondi felt the knife-edge of grief slice itself into her heart. A vital part of her had surely died with that little girl. She did not have the strength to hold baby Thokoza any more, surrendering her completely to her mother while MaZulu kept charge of the boys.

Whenever she had some store of energy, she asked to be taken for visits to MaJere, and she would come back still sick in body but with her spirits raised. With each visit to her grandmother Zondi grew to accept that she was on a journey, which everyone must make only once in a lifetime. She would not think of it as dying. She made the final flight to the other side on a peaceful afternoon in the month of June, a few days before her thirty-fifth birthday, during a visit to MaJere with her mother and Clara. The old woman, in tones beyond terrestrial comprehension, evoked in song the grace of those gone before, as her granddaughter's spirit rose on the wings of no return.

A birthday card and letter arrived for her from England a day later. Nobody had the heart to open it. Two weeks later another letter arrived. Joe opened it:

Dearest Zondi,
You didn't reply to my last mail, that is so unlike you. You will be pleased to hear that I have successfully finished my studies and will be home at the end of next month. You are the one person I look forward to seeing the most when I arrive. It has been so long since I sat and talked with you. Then you must take me to visit MaJere, one fine day. I need to touch base, as they say out here. Being with MaJere always gives back one's sense of identity. In spite of everything that is going wrong in the world today, there's so much to live for . . .
Yours truly, Thokoza

And there's so much to die for, thought Joe without sarcasm. He made a note of Thokoza's arrival date so that he would not forget to go and meet her at the airport.

Achmat Dangor
Skin Costs Extra

Simon Mashaba accepted the New York posting reluctantly. It was so inopportune, barely two months after he and Nomsa had moved into their newly acquired home on a tree-lined street in Greenside, Johannesburg. How they had looked forward to lounging by the pool that summer, reading, listening to the different texture of sounds, falling asleep in the shade of the giant old jacaranda. They had earned all of this, after enduring life in the township for so long.

He had to be in New York by the end of June, he was told. A business development position so close to the world's commercial heart could not be left vacant for long. In his heart he knew that this was an exaggeration, that he, like his predecessor, was unlikely to persuade wary investors to pour "billions" into South Africa. Why, he asked himself, could we not accept that we were an ordinary nation now that apartheid was gone, and that we had to wait our turn like the rest of Africa? He also knew that the department chief was using his appointment to soothe, for the moment, the minister's irritation at the lack of results in the US – *Mashaba knows economics, and he's one of us.*

That much was true, anyway. He was an MK soldier with an economics degree from an English university where the president had also studied. But Simon was unable to exploit either of his talents, and had become neither a general in the army nor anyone important in the ministry of finance. He was too diffident, people said, lacking in passion, and far too willing to accede to the viewpoints of others. So, at the age of fifty, he was being sent to New York to do a thankless job.

You are too generous, his wife Nomsa said when he informed her of the transfer. *With my life as well as yours*, she had added bitterly.

Nomsa had to give up her position as senior lecturer at Wits University, putting on hold the prospects of becoming a full professor. Matters became worse when she saw the documents that described her as a "dependant spouse". This was what they would stamp in her passport, for the entire world to see, especially those smug immigration officials who would smile indulgently at her: poor, helpless woman.

However, she was not the kind of person to carry on complaining about

things. After she had consented to joining Simon in New York, she resolved to make the best of things. But she told him that she needed time
to wind up her affairs at home; she would follow him to New York after
a month or so. She used the time to secure a part-time lecturer's position
at Hunter College in New York, and only told Simon about this, by telephone, once he was already there.

He left at the end of June. On an impulse, he decided to stay over with
old Sussex varsity friends who now lived near Birmingham. He was travel-
ling via London anyway. He then made an equally impulsive decision not
to go to their home, some thirty miles north of Birmingham, but to book
into a hotel in the old town. After calling his friends to make some or
other excuse, he had dinner and then went for a walk. He stopped in at a
bar for a drink where he met a young woman. He would afterwards think
of their encounter as an "adventure", during which sex was somehow offered and procured. It was dissatisfying, and left him with a feeling of
shame. She was pale and thin, insubstantial, so unlike Nomsa. The room,
a basement flat, was clean though, and light fell upon them from the street.

He tried to rationalise: this whole series of events was prompted by a
subliminal and difficult to understand impetus inside of him. Perhaps he
needed to find out whether indeed he had any passion left, whether he
still had the nerve to court danger, just like in the old days when he smug-
gled arms and scouted out military targets. In the end, he wiped away the
memory of that encounter, and proceeded to New York to start his new
life as if this diversion had never happened.

He arrived promptly, as required, on the first of July. He was surprised
by the humidity, the almost tropical feel of sweat all over his skin. Mercifully, the efficient consular staff helped him settle in quickly. Nomsa had
called to inform him of her position at Hunter College and her desire to
live in Manhattan – *so that she could at least be close to things.* He rented an
apartment on 41st Street in a place called Tudor City. He soon realised
how pretentious the surroundings were; mock turrets of white stone and a
pervasive smell of decay, stone seeped in urine. The apartment was small
compared to their Greenside home, smaller even than the Soweto house.
But it was close to the East River, and this gave it a sense of space. In the
morning, sunshine reflected off the water, gilding the edges of buildings
and turning windows into mirrors. Looming over the apartment were three
Con Edison chimney stacks on First Avenue. They provided the solidity he
craved in cities, and balanced the movie-like contrast between the decadence
of the dark buildings and the river's magical sparkle.

The chimneys towered over the horizon, and seemed part of the river's defences against encroaching humanity. He told himself that he would find out whether they still functioned. It would be a pity if they had been rendered obsolete by some new way of powering the turbines, gas for example that filled the air with invisible pollutants. What honest mechanical beasts they must once have been, unashamedly belching out the smoke of their endeavours!

Nomsa was due soon, and he had to make sure that the apartment appeared as welcoming as possible. Her tone of voice warned him to be sensitive to the sacrifice she was making. The place seemed more Spartan suddenly, so he bought a bookshelf and unpacked their books, hung the Peter Magubane photographs of Johannesburg that he had brought over, and purchased a bright Mexican mask from a downtown shop he had stumbled across.

When Nomsa arrived she seemed cheerful enough, even if her dark eyes had a familiar, and unsettling, gleam of gentleness mixed with cold resolve. Something inside her was changing. He had seen it happening before: Nomsa adjusting, slowly easing herself into the new currents of her life. The last time she had that look was when she lost the baby. He only knew she was pregnant when she started bleeding, and she told him to hurry and get her to hospital to prevent a miscarriage. They were too late.

Soon, however, they settled into a welcome rhythm in New York. He walked to his office on 37th Street each day, while she took the subway to Hunter College three times a week. They took up routines established over the years. They enjoyed an austere breakfast together of coffee and bananas, taking turns to prepare a strong, dark brew on the stove and set out the peeled fruit on a plate. It sealed their daily closeness. They also shared domestic chores, washing and cleaning, preparing dinner. Each night, they shared a ritual drink. She drank only red wine, and he beer. That, she said, was the only truly African thing about him. Both of them loved the theatre and the movies, and exploring the city, walking for miles in random directions, gradually becoming familiar with the clusters of shops, restaurants, cinemas and bookstores that New Yorkers called their neighbourhoods. They made some friends, mostly from the college where Nomsa taught. Simon rarely socialised with his colleagues, outside of official receptions. The atmosphere was too intense, he said, they all needed a break from one another.

Towards the end of August, with the first anniversary of "9/11" looming, the city was overcome by a heatwave. People moved about slowly, as if the earth's gravity had increased beyond human tolerance. This was the hottest summer in memory, people said.

That's when he saw the change in Nomsa take shape. The earlier, subtle hint in her eyes flowed down into her body so that she seemed fuller, more voluptuous. Her habits also changed. She stopped drinking alcohol, filled the bath with warm water and soaked herself for an hour each day, even though it was so hot outside that Simon could only think of plunging into an icy river. She seemed gentler somehow, but also more tired. But Simon's concern for her was overtaken by an event in his own life. He tried not to think of it as dramatic, in fact tried not to think about it all, as was his habit in the face of difficulties.

The Consulate required that he undergo a medical examination. They needed to assess how much of a "cost risk" he was, for health insurance purposes. Simon was healthy for his age, ate well and exercised regularly, and had no concerns when he went to the doctor's rooms. He overcame his discomfiture when the doctor turned out to be a woman, stripped down to his underwear and dutifully submitted to a thorough examination. She asked whether he would object to having an HIV test? It could reduce his monthly payments significantly. He agreed, and thought no more of it until she called and asked him to come and see her. She wanted to take more blood; they had to repeat the HIV test.

The first one was positive. I'm sorry.

He hardly listened to her "counselling", which he thought was ritualistic and insincere. He stared malevolently at her lips as she spoke – *look out for sudden weight loss, fungal infections, and register a treatment programme* – trying to will her to stop, hoping that the words would not leave her mouth, that they would build up and throttle her. He took the subway home, watching people secretly, to see if they were looking at him. Could they see what was inside of him, a mysterious, invisible force of death, a veritable plague. He imagined himself, his face skeletal, his eyes deep and sunken. He knew that he had to pull himself together, find the courage to tell Nomsa, the right tone of voice, the right occasion.

Then he remembered that the doctor had taken more blood and that another test was to be done. He breathed easier. He could wait. Perhaps the results of the first test were wrong; after all, the medical profession was notorious for misdiagnosing serious ailments.

But Doctor Reyna de la Madrid called again. A made-up name he thought, recalling some of the Spanish he had learned from his Cuban military instructors twenty years before. As unreal as her voice and her limp, unsympathetic eyes.

On the appointed day he was reluctant to go and see Queenie la Madrid, as he had sarcastically dubbed her. He made up mental excuses until the last minute, then took a taxi to her rooms at the Cornell Medical Centre. He lingered outside until it was almost too late, hoping that she would pass him over and take another patient. But she was waiting for him, her expression sombre, trained to give people bad news, he thought. He changed her name to Ice Queen.

I am sorry. The second test confirmed the first one.

He went home by taxi, too despondent to face the imagined scrutiny of fellow passengers on the subway. He thought back to that night in Birmingham, to the freedom he felt wandering about the old city, the chance drink in the pub on the deserted square, the first time he had gone drinking by himself since he was a student. He remembered the woman at the bar, how they talked in innuendo, hints that were both mercenary – after all a bargain was being struck – and tender. Her voice, low, controlled, when they were already undressed: *Skin costs extra.*

He moaned out loud, and the taxi driver looked at him in the mirror.

Surely it couldn't have happened, just like that, in those few minutes?

Nomsa! She had been systematically unfaithful. Well periodically. But does that not imply a pattern? And is this disease not transmitted through a pattern of sexual partners? Suddenly, he saw an explanation for the change in her. It was – this time – not just the knowledge of an infidelity weighing down on her, but the realisation of the consequences! Why didn't Nomsa confess, tell him that she had slept with another man? He had been so blind – the extra month in Johannesburg, "to wind up her affairs" . . . Now, her tiredness, her moods, her attempts to improve her resistance, giving up alcohol, eating organically grown vegetables, fish instead of meat!

He felt better. He was not the transmitter of this deadly virus after all. The thought filled him with warmth. He would be generous, and demonstrate his love. Not ask how she got infected. Say to her: I understand, these things happen. He had to wait for the right moment to confront her, as it were, with the truth and his forgiveness.

On Sunday they went for a walk, down First Avenue, along the river to the ferry and the heli-pad. They watched a helicopter land, a ferry depart. They browsed for a while in a bookshop. He suggested they go down Third Avenue, towards Union Square.

Let's find a nice place, have a drink.

At the busy intersection on 23rd Street, Nomsa paused and asked if they could turn back.

I feel so worn out.

And he could see her exhaustion in her ashen face. Black people don't go pale, he thought, we get ash in our skins. He was filled once more with a protective love. When she stopped outside a flower shop and looked inside, he gently urged her to go in. *Take a break from the heat.* It was cool inside, and clean for this part of Third Avenue. He touched the satiny surface of false flowers, and observed the leftover roses curling up, marking in his mind their churlish likeness to unhappy old people. He knew that Nomsa would shrink away from the beauty of dying things. She was not a sentimental person.

In the end they bought a single orchid that the shopkeeper wrapped up in fancy paper and cellophane. Simon insisted on paying. Twenty-five dollars. An expensive gesture, but worth watching her carry it close to herself, inhaling its rich fragrance.

It smells like a real flower.

He did not want to be a spoilsport and ask whether other flowers did not smell like flowers. The unguarded moment's acid dissolved the tenderness in him and they walked home in silence.

Nomsa put the orchid in a vase and placed it in the window. An extravagant layer of blooms, like a half-opened vulva, lips speckled with pinpricks of blood, clung to a tall sinewy green stem. But it was frail against the brutal uprightness of the power station towers outside. He looked at the flower, and she at him.

It won't last long there.

It's not meant to last long, it's a damn flower.

He was stung by her sharpness, and in response she softened her face. He felt that this was the right moment to broach the subject.

I know.

Know what?

About you.

Have you been prying?

She laughed.

All right I didn't want to tell you until I was sure.

What's so funny?

Funny? I'm pregnant Simon, we're going to have a baby!

He walked down to 37th Street, past the wrought-iron gate under FDR Drive, held his breath against the smell of piss, until he was in the park and able to breathe freely. He sat on a bench and looked across the placid river. The water slapped up against the wall, an oily, sluggish noise. It was lifeless, unlike the fierce rivers at home, always challenging the earth around them, especially man-made walls. He wondered what it would be like underwater. Dark, an acrid taste when you swallowed. He imagined himself going down with outstretched arms, Christ descending, only his hair was too short for that kind of effect. He dismissed the thought: too theatrical. He thought about Nomsa, up there in the apartment weeping, trying to decide what to do next. When she told him she was pregnant – *after all these years, Simon, it's a miracle* – she stopped laughing and giggling, and stared at him.

What did you think was the matter with me?

You looked so tired.

Well, I'm feeding another life in me.

She came closer to him.

Simon, what's wrong?

He told her about Doctor Reyna de la Madrid, about the two blood tests. She did not laugh at his feeble joke about her name, Queenie the Ice Queen, nor did she respond to the mechanical way in which he told her that he was HIV positive. She sat down on the bed, stared out of the window, tears started rolling down her cheeks. He left her there, muttering to herself, *my baby, my baby.*

He walked back towards the apartment, wondering whether Nomsa was still there. Somehow he hoped that she would be gone, that the apartment would be empty. He was tired, and longed to sink into the sheets, into the void of the river, the shadows of the three giant sentinels.

Rustum Kozain

Crossing from Solitude

The meagre sun outside I know
climbs the height of Cape Town's
odd, blue, winter sky. Inside,
we sit or lie in the fast

cooling bath, refill it again,
again, it cools again. We talk shit,
laugh, or worry, declare,
confess, tell stories. Then

we'll mob each other
like the crazed lovers we are
                    uncontained
            and certain as our bodies

seek their single truths, caring
not for anything but to cross
that silent, undeclared,
still solitude we cross now, again;

caring not for anything
but my leg in its space between
your legs; your hand on me
as if it's my hand on me

or your hand on yourself.

Later, you'll leave for a rally.
June, 16. A new fight
as our country falls again,
still, to plague and old men

muddled and muzzled by an old
God who clearly couldn't care
he gave us cocks and cunts,
arseholes, the language of the fuck,

the body's craze for assonance;
a country still in awe
of aged young lions whose deaths
give the lie to their own lies.

Your politics an ache, an anger
that two days ago unfurled
in my bathroom, and raged
against silence, against inaction –

you, apologetic as if I did not care
nor harboured aches or anger;
me, caught still in a cooling bath.
I will dawdle, then also leave

to a stack of papers, bills,
laundry, the changing politics
of my everyday that now
must struggle against your

absence, yours. A bath that cools
for no one, an odd blue sky,
the sun that falls now
towards evening, towards winter

as our confessions deepen,
declarations that circle and skirt
the unsaid of how else
the human might cross from solitude.

Lesley Emanuel
Confetti

I used to write out the death reports, referring to the medical notes and adding details from my mental picture of the patient. Now there are new forms with fields for entries, so I write *Innocent* for name, draw a line for surname, *approx. 9* for age at time of death, *LIP* for cause of death. Next to this I write out *lymphocytic interstitial pneumonitis* and bracket it.

At the end of the report form there are ten or so lines for additional notes. I can't think what to write there. A précis of who brought him in? *Elderly woman.* History of HIV/AIDS-related infections? *Seizures, fever, diarrhoea, dehydration.* Favourite toy? *Woody the Cowboy (missing one foot).*

I have a Polaroid picture of Innocent in my journal. It shows him sitting cross-legged in the dirt outside the ward. On that day I had given the children koki pens to draw faces on calabashes. Innocent was holding his calabash up and was grinning as wildly as the ghoulish face he had drawn. He was very small. In the picture, the bulb of the calabash is only a little smaller than his head. He was always cold. We had found a woollen glove for him to wear upended on his head – he's wearing it in the picture. I can't remember where we got such a thing in this tropical country, perhaps from one of the staff members who had just arrived from Europe. The glove was stretched to fit over Innocent's forehead and when he slid down into the bed, all you'd see were five empty fingers at the top of the sheet, like a high-five signal while he was sleeping.

I gem-clip the picture to the death report.

Someone in the camp is playing a radio, there's a soccer game on. I still think of this as a camp, which is what it was when I arrived here. Now we have two more army tents and a brand-new building for Paediatric AIDS. The soccer commentator's voice rises with excitement, then it's suddenly silenced. Naomi probably had it turned off, it's Sunday after all – and I remember we have a meeting, scheduled outside because Naomi seems to think that sitting under a tree will be a relaxing way for us to talk about the trials and despondencies of our work.

While I finish Innocent's death report and file it, I think of home, of walking down to the pub for a drink with my mates on a Sunday, and of taking turns to bemoan work and Mondays.

"L'Umbelico del Mondo" is painted on the door of the Land Rover, the text in a crescent around Venus de Milo's navel. The vehicle was donated by an Italian popstar who has a hit single about the belly button of the world. Naomi has adopted the name for our camp, because of its connotations of birth and motherhood. One of the other healthworkers, who admitted defeat by dust and depression, coloured in the navel with a black marker before he went home. So it's a grimy belly button now.

Naomi is sitting on a box of HIV/AIDS pamphlets, resting her back against the Land Rover with her legs spread to get the best possible draught. She's a great believer in calamine lotion, smears it up there for relief against the chafing. I'm picturing the congealed, dried pink stuff on Naomi's inner thighs and I only catch the tail-end of what she is saying, something about AIDS education.

"Health workers are educators. Educators are liberators. It's through the word – the printed word – the leaflets, that we can, that we will, educate. What is the point, you have to ask, what is the point finally, in handing out condoms when we don't look at the real problem?"

I look across the circle. Zadie, fresh in from UNAIDS, is shadowing a fly with her hand, inching up to where it has settled on her shoulder, then clutching at it. No luck. Naomi's voice has settled into a thick, slow drone. I'm drawing circles in the dirt with my big toe.

"The real problem . . ." Naomi pauses for effect – "the real problem is a lack of context and understanding. When we understand what these people's lives are like, we'll be able to make a difference. Which brings me to the pamphlets."

Naomi heaves forward and points at an opened leaflet.

"They've been designed to educate in pictures. And look, the pictures are of rural scenes, so our people can identify. Now you can use them to explain the consequences of unprotected sex. Just yesterday I had a group sitting around me as you are now. They left, each with a load of leaflets, to spread the information."

So that's where the three giggling boys passing my tent yesterday had come from.

"OK," Naomi sighs, "a box each, please, to be circulated to all the mothers you see, by next week. I don't think that's too much to ask."

She closes the leaflet in front of her.

"And for those of you who want to attend service, it'll be after the wedding tonight. I don't suppose there will be many people, there's bound to be a big party with all this going on."

She waves an arm in the direction of the valley.

Everyone in the meeting turns to look down to the valley below our camp. People are making their way to the church in the village. There is laughing and a woman ululates. The colours of their clothes are brilliant on this bright, hot afternoon. I scan the group quickly to gauge their interest. We'll all be going down, surely, to break the tedium. I need to wash my feet.

I walk with Zadie to show her the path.

"I've never been to a wedding in Africa before," I tell her.

"I've never been *anywhere* in Africa before," she replies.

She's American and she says "anywhere" with a long drawl. She arrived about a month ago and we still haven't had a chance to chat much, but I think I'll like Zadie. She has a fresh, open face and that enthusiasm young, newly qualified people have about working with HIV-infected patients. Somewhere behind us, music from a ghetto blaster distorts, dips and rises with the person carrying it down the uneven path.

As we walk towards the first knots of people, the song finds its wavelength, settling into a rhythmic throb. The people around Zadie and I are silent, they look at us and quickly turn away. A man points at me, then gives an order to the ghetto blaster owner, who turns the sound down. I realise that I'm the reminder of Innocent's death.

I recognise young mothers, babies on their hips, who have been to the clinic. A photographer in a three-piece suit, sweat streaming from under his hat and rolling down his face, is setting up a tripod. Boys are watching him with their mouths open and their hands on their hips. I'm standing too close to an unwashed body, acrid stink wafts in my direction. I move off towards three women in hats and shiny starched pleats. They stare, smile, turn to each other, talk in hushed tones. One of them finally says, "Hello, Sister," and pushes her baby at me.

I'm happy to have something to hold. It makes me feel less spare. The baby has rubbery leg-wrinkles and a fat tummy that folds solidly onto the top of his thighs. He makes a shiny spit bubble and laughs when it pops. The late afternoon sun feels good on the back of my neck. I can see into the heart of the crowds, to a man with his head back, guffawing. There's a woman admiring her friend's earrings and a young teenage girl winding through the crowd, carefully carrying a glass of water. She has one hand around the glass, the other beneath it; she dips her knees as she hands it to an old woman. The woman touches the girl's cheek and leaves her hand there for a moment.

The crowd thickens and bodies press together. Ululations trill over all our heads like a wave. I'm nudged, pushed and then together we all surge forward: the bride has arrived! She steps out of a black Mercedes, ignores the pandemonium, the crescendo of shouts and whoops, and looks instead at the back of her dress to make sure it isn't caught in the door. She is a vision, a hologram of white satin with a blue sheen in the bright light, emphasised by her black skin and the polished car. She lowers her eyes demurely and studies her white silk roses, picking at the yellowing parts. Then she rests a hand on her pregnant stomach, arches her back, and sways to the church door. I hear her dress crackle as she walks past my section of the crowd. The satin pulls at her belly and tightens over the swell of it so that her navel protrudes. I think how her belly button will be the first part of her into the church.

Zadie is touching my elbow, trying to get my attention. I had forgotten about her, with the baby and the noise.

"Liz!" she says urgently, "Liz, that woman – the bride – I recognise her – I tested her two weeks ago . . ." I have to lean closer to hear her over the noise, "and she's positive."

We watch the bride's back being swallowed up by the darkness of the church interior.

Zadie says, "Oh hell, do you think the groom knows?"

The baby's mother must have made it into the press of the church. I'm wondering how long the ceremony will be, how long before the mother claims her child back. Zadie has headed off, returned to the camp. We loiter about – me, the baby and the others who didn't commandeer seats at lunchtime. Perhaps just as well: the sounds of singing and stomping from the church are continuous and I'm glad I'm not in there. The sun is dropping; a few scrawny chickens survey the emptied lot around the church for debris. The baby is settled, playing with some beads around my neck.

It's a brief calm, then the bride and her new husband emerge from the church, and we're in the thick of it again. The crowd is even hotter now, bodies warmed from the close space inside. I see the groom for the first time, not anything as spectacular as his wife. He is wearing dirty tennis shoes and his shirt collar is too big. Two small girls hold up baskets, garnished with orange florist's ribbon, their arms straight up so that the grown-ups don't need to bend down to them. The men scoop up the confetti, the ladies take little amounts between fingers like pincers and the children have their hands smacked away. Everyone tries to get at the baskets, it's only the bearers who aren't smiling. The bride ducks charmingly at the paper shower and her husband grins and shouts a good-humoured insult at one of his friends.

76

I'm standing away from the crowd but some confetti floats towards me, carried on the enthusiasm of the crowd and the only breeze of the afternoon. Some of it settles on the baby's shoulders and forehead. He gurgles and smiles happily at the bits of paper.

"Yes," I say, and jostle him a bit, "your mama's coming, see? Here she comes . . ."

His mother approaches us, smiling and holding out her hands to the baby. Her face is shiny and her skirt pleats are limp. I lick a finger and press it to one of the confetti bits, tidying the baby for her. Just before I blow it away, I recognise the fragment of text printed on it. It is from one of Naomi's pamphlets: *HIV*.

Kay Brown

The Harvest

I stop at the home industry shop and buy a cake. Lemon and poppy seed sounds the most nutritious, so I choose that. Also two cans of fizzy drink, because he's always thirsty.

The hospital is a maze of low bungalows. I park the car and walk down a corridor, past the sign that says *"ISOLATION"* and into the first ward. There is only one patient in the room. He is lying on top of the bedclothes with his eyes shut. One hand is curled on his chest, as dry and insubstantial as an autumn leaf.

"Langton?"

He struggles to sit. He speaks to me, but the words are a meaningless jumble of English and Sotho. They echo in the stark, barren room. He drinks a can of cold drink without stopping, soaking it up through the straw. I offer him a piece of cake and he nods. I go to find the nurse, to get a knife and a plate. She is wheeling a metal cabinet down the passage, dispensing pills. "Not now," she says, in a tone that implies *not ever*. So I sit on a flimsy plastic chair, hack off a piece of cake with my penknife and hand it to him. His hospital pyjamas have blue stripes and are scrunched up to the knees. His legs dangle down like dark, thin aerial roots.

"I had to get a plumber," I tell him. "Two hundred and fifty rand just to tell me the problem with the geyser was electrical. I'm battling without you."

He smiles, but his eyes are dull and uncomprehending.

"All the front units were flooded again," I say, still hoping for a response.

He puts a piece of cake into his mouth and eats it slowly. Tiny black poppy seeds stick between his teeth and cling to the moisture on his lip. He watches me, as remote now as when he watched me years ago, when he was Nick's "boy".

Nick was the maintenance manager. He leaned against his bakkie, cigarette in hand.

"That guy who runs the bakery hasn't got the window fixed. Says it's your problem."

Nick was a chain-smoker. His fingers were stained the colour of butternut.

"It's in his lease," I replied. "He's responsible for maintenance of everything except the roof."

"Bugger says he didn't break it." Nick sucked at his cigarette and wheezed. "Attempted break-in."

"I'll speak to him. If he'll pay for the glass we'll do the repair."

I knew the tenant would be happy with the compromise. My job was negotiating between the property owner and the tenants, passing instructions down to Nick. But Langton would be the one who would replace the glass, breaking out the damaged pane, smoothing new putty into the corners. He was the one who had the youth and strength to dig down to a broken pipe, or to climb on a roof to mend a leak. He was the one who could be trusted to paint areas no one else would ever see.

As years went by the cigarettes slowly sucked the life out of Nick, until he could no longer work. I went to say goodbye. Langton helped him pack his personal tools into his bakkie.

"Ma'am, please may I speak with you," said Langton after Nick had left and we were standing alone in the workshop.

Langton wore a knitted cap, summer or winter, and this was the first time I had ever seen him take it off. He twisted it between his hands.

"I can do the work. No problem. I have been doing the work now for many, many weeks, since Master Nick has been ill."

He put his hat down on the workbench and picked up a couple of papers, which he handed to me. He had already taken all the meter readings. And he had the debtor's list up to date. As each tenant had paid he had ticked the amount off with a back to front tick in the left margin. Nick was left-handed and made his ticks that way.

Langton had been watching and learning, storing knowledge quietly, patiently hoping for the right conditions, like a desert flower that stays dormant for years, seemingly lifeless, before the rains come and it bursts into bloom.

"I'll speak to the boss," I promised.

The owner was hesitant. "He'll need a driver's licence," he said.

So I arranged for Langton to have lessons and he passed at the first attempt.

"He doesn't have his own transport," the owner said.

I put in a motivation for a second-hand vehicle we could keep on site.

"WELCOME, FORD 3000" Langton wrote in large, bold letters across his timesheet when the battered bakkie arrived. I felt a personal triumph.

"There is no need for you to come every day," he said, after the first months had passed. "I'll do the banking for you. Just show me how to fill in the form."

"Any problems?" I asked when I phoned.

"No. No problems this side. The harvest has been good."

"The harvest?"

"Yes. Our harvest is the money. You give me the statements, the seeds, and I take care of the harvest."

"I like that," I said. I could hear him chuckle.

"Now everyone has paid but unit nineteen. He's been arrested for the murder of his wife."

"Good grief! He killed her?"

"No. The police think so, because she was bruised. But it was alcohol that killed her. Looking too deep in the bottle. I think they will release him soon. Oh, and I have found a tenant for unit five. A lady who sells groceries. Also toilet paper, which is good. We use more toilet paper every month and she sells at a discount."

Langton has picked up the second can. He holds it carefully with both hands.

"Shall I open it?" I ask. He smiles and nods, but he keeps clutching it when I reach for it. I feel his confusion and do not know what to do next. I can hear the distant noise of television from another ward. "Soccer," I say, pointing in the direction of the sound. "I think Pirates are playing." He has supported the team passionately for years; maybe a remnant of that enthusiasm can get through to him. But he doesn't seem to hear. He takes one hand off the can and wipes the dampness down the front of his pyjama top.

He has TB and meningitis. I looked at his file a few weeks ago, when I was alone for a moment in the nurse's office. The TB he has had for over a year. But the word "meningitis" sent me scrabbling anxiously for information. The articles I read stated it was very rare unless in someone whose natural immunity has been impaired by age, by drugs such as cortisone, or by the HIV virus. Scary information.

Useless information.

"Langton, how many years have we worked together now?"

"Since 1 October, 1991. Nick left December 1997."

"Over a decade. That's a long time. We're a good team, you and I. I need you. All this talk of HIV has me worried. If there's a problem, I'll help you."

"No problem. It was just TB. The pills I'm drinking are making me strong again."

He didn't look strong. He had his own second-in-command now and there were days he let that young man do all the work.

"But it's better to be sure, huh? Maybe it would be a good idea to have a test."

"No, no. They did a test. After that last time at the hospital. HIV negative. No problem."

No problem? Each month, little by little, his energy drained and his body withered.

I join the queue to speak to the doctor. There are five of us waiting, all squeezed together on a narrow bench. There are posters on the wall about HIV. They tell me nothing I don't already know, but I stare at the pictures.

I had been hurt and angry at Langton's denials. If you don't acknowledge something how can you fight it? But as I sit there I wonder how on earth you can acknowledge something you cannot see. A virus is such a little thing. So incomprehensibly tiny. How can something so small wreak such havoc? How could it have cut down a man in his prime?

The doctor is tall and stooped. He shakes my hand when I walk in, looks me in the eye. He smells of disinfectant.

"You are not a member of the family." It was a statement, not a question.

"No, a colleague," I reply. I choose the word carefully. Perhaps for a colleague the rules of confidentiality don't apply. Perhaps this time, with this doctor, I can be persuasive enough. "Is there anything I can do? He seems to be getting worse."

"He is. I'm discharging him."

"But he's still so ill!"

"Yes, I know that. There is nothing more we can do. His wife was here this morning. He is going home today."

The room is suddenly icy cold. My hands are trembling.

"Surely there is something else you can do . . . some other medication? His employer will pay for it."

He shakes his head. "Miracles happen, but barring that he won't be back at work." He opens the door, beckons to the next person sitting on the bench. For a moment I cannot move.

"I'm very sorry," he says.

Tears have blocked my throat and I can't speak. I do not look at him as I pass.

I return to Langton's room. He's still perched on the edge of the bed. His relatives will be fetching him soon, taking him home. I sit down to wait for them. I must discuss the awful, final practicalities – send my condolences to his children. He was so proud of them. What does the future hold for them now?

I think of the tractor he bought, that he was taking home at Christmas, and of the land he was hoping to get.

I remember words from *The Rubáiyát of Omar Khayyám*:

> *With them the Seed of Wisdom did I sow,*
> *And with my own hand labour'd it to grow;*
> *And this was all the Harvest that I reap'd –*
> *"I came like Water, and like Wind I go."*

I start to cry. My head sinks onto my chest so that all I can see are his dangling feet. He will die before they can reach the soil. This is not the way it should have been. When you sow in sorrow, you should reap in joy.

I mourn for him, and for our blighted harvest.

Edward Chinhanhu
Our Christmas Reunion

The day was December 24th, and Selby was coming home. I'd done well at school, the rains had been excellent and, to top it all, Selby was coming home. Nothing, absolutely nothing in this world could beat the sweet, joyful anticipation that filled my soul at my big brother's homecoming, and, of course, the prospects of a bountiful harvest. He had already sent the money to buy a goat for Christmas, and I had obliged by selecting a huge one that, on this penultimate day itself, I was busy skinning on the veranda of a disused old shed.

You see, we were poor peasants, and my ageing mother and I had lived deep in the sequestered, mountainous village of Matida for as long as my mother's memory could stretch, tilling the hard, rocky ground whose yield seemed to dwindle year after year. Father had long since drowned in the nearby Mutorahuku, drunk as ever, after a heated quarrel with mother. After father's death mother wore no other colour but black, and I had vowed never to touch alcohol for as long as I lived. Now, at eighteen, I was still resolute about that. When father died, Selby had just completed Form Three at one of those now defunct, hastily constructed, under-funded secondary schools built at independence and generically called "upper-tops". This one had been taken over by a group of zealous Catholic missionaries and nuns. I was three or four then.

We were the only children in the family and the bond between us was stronger than that of any two siblings who had ever walked the earth, despite the wide gap in our ages. I worshipped the ground Selby walked on. From the tender age of two, I would accompany him everywhere he went, and that included school, sometimes. With my thumb firmly stuck in my mouth, I would spend the day with his class, ignoring the discouraging comments and innocuous jokes from his mates and teachers.

Today, however, when I look back on the embarrassment I might have caused him, I feel like sinking into the ground with shame.

But Selby didn't seem to mind. We would go fishing together, we mended mother's fence together, we watered the garden together, bathed in the Mutorahuku together, fetched water, ate from the same plate, played, sang, laughed and cried together, my big brother and I. We slept between the same blankets, which I inevitably soiled from time to time.

And then he went to London. Ah, but more about that later.

First, here is an incident that sticks vividly in my mind and which I believe has a symbiotic relationship with the tale I want to tell. It was around midday and, having fallen out with my regular playmates, I decided to wander along the Mutorahuku. About three hundred metres downstream I changed course and made a sudden turn towards the nearby school grounds. I could see people there, and I hoped Selby would be among them.

I emptied my pockets of the pebbles I'd picked up on my excursion along the river, my mind vaguely trying to cook up an excuse for my unexpected appearance at school. Soon, panting for breath, I was in the playground, where a few dozen people either sprawled on the turf perusing books, or milled about enjoying the June sun. To the left, near the football goalposts, was a knot of six or seven boys, apparently engrossed in something I was too far away to see.

My eyes scanned the playground for my brother and, failing to see him anywhere else, I made for the standing group. About thirty metres away, I spotted him. His back was towards me. I ran again, and soon was upon them. Playfully, I tugged at Selby's shorts, and he turned.

"He-e-y!" he exclaimed gleefully, bending down and throwing a loose arm around my neck. "Howzeta m'face?" We went through our own greeting rigmarole – touching fingers and thumbs, rather too quickly, I thought. Selby once again swung his arm around my neck, pulled me to him, and then returned his attention to whatever it was he was discussing with his friends. Gently, I squeezed my body between him and another boy to see what it was that could take Selby's attention from me.

At the centre of the circle stood a boy, bright-eyed, with an unmistakably mischievous mouth. He held a shaved stick in one hand and a rolled-up plastic tube (it looked like a balloon to me) in another. He was explaining something to the group, who all were laughing, clapping and shaking hands. The boy rolled the plastic tube up the stick.

"You see," he was saying, "You do it carefully, slowly – or better still, you make her roll it up. Make her. . ."

Suddenly a female voice broke in, "What do you think you're doing, boys?"

Every head turned, and fear-filled eyes rested on a short, plump, bespectacled woman in Catholic regalia. She had a cane in one hand.

Quickly, the circle dissolved, and the boys leaped out of the cane's reach. The boy who held the plastic-wrapped stick tried to shake off the plastic, at the same time trying to flee. After three quick shakes it came off, but instead of falling to the ground it flew onto my chest and stuck there.

Gripped with fear, I jumped and screamed, using my fingers to try and toss it off. While engaged in this frantic effort, rough hands seized me. This threw me into a deeper, frenzied panic.

"Whose child is this?" shrieked the woman, her face horrified.

No one answered. Selby had moved a short distance away and was watching from there.

"I said whose child is this," she repeated shrilly.

Again Selby did not answer.

She pulled me towards a piece of paper lying on the grass and, to protect her hands, used it to pick the plastic off my shirt.

"The owner of this child will have to follow me to the headmaster's office. That's where he will pick him up."

With that she swung me around and force-marched me towards the school buildings. I cried, but she took no heed.

Then Selby was upon us.

"Madame," he said in his usual polite tone, "he's my young brother."

She stopped walking, still holding me firmly by the shoulder, and looked directly into Selby's eyes.

"You!" she spat, "you're a prefect aren't you? And you bring such filthy things into our school?"

"No, Madame Sister . . ."

"Do you know that this is a clean Catholic school, a godly, holy institution?" She was beside herself with rage. "I can't let this pass," she continued, sinking her knuckles into my collarbone as she pulled me along.

Selby fell in step with us.

"No, Madame Sister. Do not drag him. I'll carry him to the office myself."

But the woman wouldn't listen.

Selby's proximity pacified me somewhat, and I did not resist. My crying too subsided. Still, I couldn't make sense of anything. We reached the door to the headmaster's office and blew in like a hurricane.

"Headmaster . . ." she panted.

But there was no one in. She swung around, and zoomed out again, pulling me with her. We went past one classroom, and another, then we saw the headmaster in the third, teaching a class. He was a grey-haired man with a kindly, fatherly look. Again we barged in.

"Headmaster," said the nun, "can you believe this? Look! Just look at how . . ."

The rest of her words were drowned out by stifled bursts of laughter from the class because, as she ranted, she dangled the plastic in the air, and it swung to and fro like a tired pendulum. The headmaster looked on stonily, unblinking. He looked from the nun to me, and finally, almost inaudibly he said, "Follow me." We all followed him to the office, the nun bringing up the rear. Once inside, the headmaster looked at Selby, his eyes boring into him.

"Is that thing yours?" he asked.

"No, Sir," Selby answered.

"Liar!" shouted the nun, pointing a shaking finger at him.

"It's not mine, Sir. Somebody picked it up on the playing field."

"Who?"

"I cannot remember. We were playing on the field, and . . ."

"Go and call your parents," ordered the headmaster, sitting down.

"Please, Sir. I only have my mother. She's sick and she cannot . . ."

"Then we will have to expel you from school. This is a very serious offence. The authorities will simply not let it pass. Either you call your mother here and we talk to her, or you have to withdraw. No exams."

Selby had no option but to call mother to school. I wasn't privy to what followed, but what I clearly remember, even to this day, is my mother crying her heart and eyes out. For days she did not eat. Nor did Selby.

They were still bent on expelling Selby, and for five days he did not attend school. Later, however, the headmaster relented and allowed him back. He was punished and lost his position as prefect. For a long time he was viewed with suspicion by the nuns and brothers who ran the school, as well as by other students, but he never gave his friends away. They secretly admired and praised him. I know this because they came to prepare for their exams at our house at night. I knew that I was somehow to blame for my brother's misery, and that had I not been on the grounds that day Selby would have escaped the nun and everything brought upon him. But he never mentioned this. He still loved me as he had before.

He passed his Form Four well enough, and proceeded to a different school for his A-Levels, on a generous scholarship from a local tea company. He passed these with glee, and everyone – teachers, sisters, friends, priests – all came to our dilapidated home to congratulate him, his past wrongs totally forgotten.

And then he went to London.

I cannot describe in enough detail how his departure affected me. I had no idea of journeys and distances, and London might as well have been a kilometre or two away, but the fact that Selby was going somewhere without me gnawed at the very roots of my soul. When he did not come home that first evening, I felt like my world had crumbled all around me.

I sobbed the whole night, and on countless others after it. It was a month before I eventually accepted the letters he wrote every week, and agreed to look at the photographs he sent us. Mother read the letters to me with hilarious, exaggerated elaborations. With time, I treasured these letters the way Jews treasured their early scriptural writings. They were the only bond now between Selby and me. I pored over them till I could identify each of them by a smudge, or a folded corner, a peculiar crease or stain, and could recite all that they said, sentence by sentence, without looking or reading. Mother chastised me for carrying them to school, but still I managed to sneak one or two in my pocket from time to time to show my friends.

When Selby returned from London, he secured a big job with a bank in Harare, and for the past two years had been working there. Of course, he did come home from time to time, but not as often as we all wanted. He paid my fees at a good boarding school, and built two new houses to expand our homestead. Life was comfortable. The love we had for each other did not change, only matured and grew less selfish (especially on my part). Selby was more than a brother to me, and more than a son to my mother now. He was our refuge, our father and lifeline, the umbilical cord that sustained our livelihood. And this was going to be our first Real Christmas with him since his return from London. I was excited, I was ecstatic, I could have touched the sky with joy. I hummed a tune under my breath as I skinned the big goat.

On that morning the rain poured incessantly, pounding the saturated earth with heavy droplets, each like the fist of a bully. There was water and mud everywhere, and the local folk revelled in it. No amount of rain, however, could deter me from meeting my brother at the bus station. When I heard the groaning and grunting of the bus as it climbed the ascent of "pagomba", I covered the carcass of the goat with sheets of plastic, placed a big dish on top and covered my head with an old yellow fertiliser container. I shouted to my mother that the bus had come, and not knowing that I still held the knife in my bloody hands, plunged into the rain. I only noticed the knife and my blood-soaked hands halfway on the journey, and cleaned them in puddles of water that collected on the road. I hid the knife in the back pocket of my khaki shorts.

I turned a corner onto the main road and, sure enough, the bus was already there at the station, a hundred metres away. There was a sizeable crowd, and much excited jumping and skipping and embracing. Shouts of laughter could be heard from quite a distance away.

When I arrived, I did not see Selby among the disembarked passengers.

With my heart beating fast, I looked frantically here and there, in front of the bus and behind it – twice. For some stupid reason, I even looked under the bus, but of course my brother wasn't there, and no one had seen him. Stinging tears began to well up in my eyes. The bus conductor hit the door of the bus with a clenched fist, signalling its departure, and slowly it moved out of our station.

Then a bell rang, and I heard someone shout, "There is somebody disembarking!" Despite my tears, I craned my neck and peered through the windows and door of the packed bus. A familiar figure was slowly making his way towards the exit, squeezing through the small spaces created for him by the noisy standing passengers, and pieces of luggage piled on the floor of the bus. As the figure drew nearer to the door, he became less and less like Selby.

With some effort and a little help from the conductor, he landed on terra firma. I came up close to him. No, he wasn't my brother Selby.

Too dark, too thin.

Yet it was him. Even before the flashy smile came, I knew it was Selby alright, my dear brother Selby. But what had happened? Instead of asking him that question, I threw myself at him, perhaps with half an intention of covering him up. We staggered a bit in the mud, but regained our balance and held each other tightly, our eyes closed, floating in space for a while.

When we released each other, I realised that the rain had stopped, and quite a crowd had gathered around us. People were peering unashamedly into my brother's face with questioning eyes. Some even hazarded the question, "Is this Selby? Really?" But my brother, with an effort that showed bravery, his eyes still shining, said, "I'm not well, Tawanda." The crowd must have understood, for slowly they turned away, but not without stealing glances at him and whispering in undertones.

We started for home. He had no luggage and, under the circumstances, I did not ask for or expect any. His walk was slow and laboured, and from time to time we stopped so that he might regain his breath. I will never forget the precious quality of that walk home. I felt very close to my brother on that day and our intimacy was a consummation of all we had ever shared.

Eventually we came to the shed where I had been skinning the goat. I cast my eyes towards the dish, and was surprised to see it flipped open, and the plastic sheets scattered all over the veranda, and even out in the mud. Then I saw dogs, quite a pack of them, tearing huge chunks of the goat meat, and running all over the place. I stood rooted, too shocked to move. I then lifted one of the plastic sheets. A heavy, dark cloud of flies rose into the air, buzzing around our faces. I looked up to my brother, but he seemed not to notice anything.

"The goat, it's been eaten," I tried to explain, but his mind was obviously preoccupied. Then slowly he turned to me and said, "Tawanda, do you know anything about AIDS?"

Then I understood, but was so stunned that even the hardest blow could not have achieved a more paralysing effect. I looked up at him, I couldn't speak. Suddenly I felt weak, and the world began to go round and round before my eyes. I fell down in a heap on the muddy ground. When I came to, I found that I was in my mother's bed, with my aunts and uncles about me. Mother wasn't there, nor was Selby.

"Your mother has gone out to the river to look for some medicine for your brother," my uncle said.

"How is that?" I asked, the energy beginning to flow back into my body.

They explained to me that my mother had become frantic at the sight of Selby. Filled with fright, she had bolted from the house, saying she knew where to find the medicine to cure what ailed her son.

Without spending words and time, let me say straight out that none of us ever saw my mother again. We walked the length and breadth of the now mighty Mutorahuku, searching and searching, but to no avail. There were no forests nearby, so we confined our search to the river. Where did we not seek, and who did not come? Even her distant relatives, some of whom we had not met but only heard of, came from various corners of the country to help in the search. There was quite a crowd at our homestead, and the rain having ceased, large fires were lit throughout the long nights. I was treated with unusual kindness throughout this whole period, though strange glances were cast at me. I also often stumbled upon unpalatable conversations about my family, but I steeled myself against it all. The deepest pain I suffered was that of being kept away from my brother as he lay quietly in his bed. His health had suddenly worsened after mother's disappearance, and he could neither eat nor drink.

So Christmas Day passed unnoticed and uncelebrated. On the 29th of December, my aunt whispered to me that my brother was in deep pain and had softly breathed my name. Upon request, I was allowed to enter his room, and hold his hand.

After about twenty minutes, my uncle said, "He's gone," and told me to release his hand.

Teboho Raboko

Sefela – Migrant Worker's Poem

(excerpt)

Greetings to you Thin Death, cow of Raboko
Illness that crossed the seas by ship
Illness that has escaped from Russia
From the Russian ships it was scaled
It came in through Maseru, place-of-the-red-sandstone,
at Mejametalana
At the very noon time
When women take their porridge pots from the fire
Removing cooking pots of sour porridge for the evening
AmaXhosa call it kill-all
Basotho call it the lying-on-the-back-disease
Young unmarried women died with their breasts out
Men died with their chests out
You can imagine how cruel the disease was
The star-faced one, yellow in colour
That white sock ill befits you
It ill befits you because it is soiled with mud
It goes out to cover this beast of my family
It goes out to cover from Motaeman's village.
It comes from Nonkokolosa
It comes from Marotobolosa
It comes from Nonthoboro
It comes from Namalibuletse
From large cities only
Where men are sickly
Where women are also sickly
Even their babies are born sickly
They speak through calabashes.

Recorded and transcribed by 'Makali I. P. Mokitimi, Monyane Mokitimi and Molefi Mokitimi. Translated from Sesotho by 'Makali I. P. Mokitimi and J. K. Matsaba.

Khaya Gqibitole

Fresh Scars

The sky was blue, the bluest I had ever seen. In the east the rising light of umsobomvu's crimson belt hugged the horizon. I could see birds going about their early morning search for food. In fact they were not even searching, there was plenty after the good early spring rains. I watched them and envied their freedom, their playfulness and their grace. My spirit lifted, opened its wings and soared with them. From my aerial view I could see the flowing rivers, tranquil mountains, cattle and sheep grazing lazily and an army of butterflies. And then, in the distance, like a bolt from the blue, I saw thousands of small white crosses.

I must have dozed off because when I opened my eyes he was standing over me. With his arms hanging loosely and his shoulders hunched, he stared right through me with misty eyes. His clothes looked loose and tired, as if he'd been walking for days. His shoes were wrinkled like an empty packet of cigarettes and he wore a hat with a lone black plume of an unrecognisable bird. He stood there for ages, frozen like a dead locust on a stem of grass.

I shivered at the thought of death and averted my gaze from the phantom shadow of my friend. At a distance I saw a huge chimney pouring black smoke up into the sky. A dark speck of cloud was beginning to form – slowly soiling the blue of the sky.

After what seemed like eternity he moved, or so I thought. I started, but quickly checked my instinct to scurry away. He proffered a skeletal hand which, when I took it in mine, felt as cold as a corpse. He smiled briefly and then slowly, almost stealthily, sat on the wooden block next to me. Now I could see the deep wrinkles that ran down his cheeks like scars. The sadness in his eyes matched that of my favourite bull, grazing nearby. I turned away from Jola and watched the bull as it gave a low bellow and galloped away. For a moment it felt as though the earth would burst open and spill out the dead.

"Jola, let me bring you amarhewu, you look tired," I said, trying to break the agonising silence.

He did not say anything and I said nothing more. I waited.

After taking a mouthful of the fermented mielie meal he smiled, displaying a set of teeth that were as white as old bones. I remembered that he never smoked or drank alcohol, something that, when we were young, seemed to give him an advantage over us as far as girls were concerned.

Then he relayed the most chilling story I had ever heard.

"Ntanga, ubom bundohlule – brother, life has defeated me," he said.

"What are you telling me now, Jola? I did not even know that you were back from Matatiele," I said, shocked.

"I am back, Dlangamandla. Home to die," he said with a bowed head.

I think I heard him swallow a tear. I knew then that there was something terribly wrong with my friend. He wanted to confide in me. Despite the beautiful sun, I was cold to the bone. The black cloud had grown tenfold by now and was moving menacingly across the sky.

"I came back last night, ntanga. It was too late to come and see you," he continued.

"After six months away from home you must have missed your family," I said, trying to sound normal. There was something disconcerting about his voice. It sounded hollow and colourless.

"How is the road construction going?" I asked mechanically.

"We are doing fine, but . . ." he sniffed, holding back tears.

"Jola, have you seen your family yet? Is everybody okay at home?"

In truth, I had already known something was wrong. MaMqocwa, his wife, had shut herself into a shell and was not visiting anyone these days. We were getting used to this change although we could not explain it. She had been an outgoing, happy and sprightly woman who was liked by everybody, a bright light that illuminated the whole village. Overnight the light had disappeared and left the village in darkness. All the self-help projects she had initiated with her husband just folded their wings and died.

In his day, Jola was a giant of a man. When we were growing up he liked sport, especially rugby. What a great tackler he was! He also excelled in maths and science, perhaps not because he was brighter but because he worked harder than the rest of us. Unfortunately, though, like all of us, his dreams were not realised. When we finished school our parents could not send us to university. We all went in different directions to earn a living.

Jola worked for a road construction company for many years. After he lost his job he did not despair but instead had rounded up a few of the local men and started repairing the village roads. Soon his workforce grew and they managed to build roads to two schools, the clinic and the local store. This was a great achievement and life in the village improved immensely. I had never thought that a mere road could so change our lives.

When the government began the Reconstruction and Development Programme, tenders were given out for a number of projects, including road construction. Big companies had to form partnerships with small black-owned companies as part of black economic empowerment. Jola was snatched up by the company that won the tender to build the Kokstad-Mount Fletcher road. Since then he had been the pride of our village. A man who put our name on the map, a man who had given hope to many. But now he says he is a defeated man!

Jola reached into his pocket and took out a packet of tobacco. This had become a ritual between us; whenever he came back he brought me Horse Shoe tobacco. He handed it to me with unsteady hands, a smile dancing on his lips. I took it and thanked him although I knew it would worsen my cough.

"Dlangamandla, life has defeated me," he said again, looking at the dis-appearing sun as if to find an explanation. "You know where we come from together. So I will not go into that now. I will start at a time when my life began to change. I am telling you this because you are the only person I can talk to now. You are the only person whose advice I value. I am telling you this dark tale because I want to take it out of my chest. And perhaps I want some help."

Now he appeared more distant and thoughtful.

"You are the first person I told when I decided to take a wife. When I took that decision I knew that it was the most important one I would ever make. At that time I thought I would be the happiest man alive, forever. That was not to be."

I topped and lit my pipe, more out of duty than need. The wind was mysteriously still and the smoke hung between us like dancing spirits.

"To be honest, I loved my wife and still do," – he darted a guilty look in the direction of his home – "but things did not go the way I thought they would. I wanted to have a big family like my father. When my first daughter was born I was happy and worked even harder to make sure that she got the best out of life. Then the second, third and fourth came along – all girls. I was devastated. I needed a son, Dlangamandla, someone to carry the family name forward. I love my daughters, there is no doubt about that, but the truth is I needed a son. Everyone in the village had a son but me."

Jola smiled in a sinister manner. I shivered.

"My wife was aware of my unhappiness and that saddened me even more. I was not blaming anyone, especially not her. When she fell preg-nant again we wanted to know the sex of the baby and so we went for a scan. Although I felt we were going against nature and culture I just wanted to know. Money can make you do these things, Dlangamandla. And guess what? It was a boy! When I heard that, I knew my prayers had been answered. I wanted to slaughter a goat in thanksgiving but I had to go back to work. For a few weeks I worked with a song in my heart. My happiness rubbed off on my men and we worked with renewed vigour."

He finished the amarhewu and put the jug on its side, indicating to me that it was empty. I knew that I had to fill it up. When I returned he was half-asleep on the grass, balancing his weight on his elbow. I gave him the jug of amarhewu and sat down on my block.

He looked at me, then said, "Dlangamandla, money can change you. It can make you do things you never thought you were capable of. But I tried not to change. I wanted to be part of my people, to be their servant. In return, they gave me love and respect. Without my people I could have done nothing."

I wanted to say something but he raised his hand to stop me.

"Dlangamandla, I am not a saint. I have made my mistakes and I regret them."

The sun was playing hide and seek in the sky, casting moving shadows on the ground. Jola's face became grave as he stared into the space between us. For a while he was so still I became concerned. Was he in a trance? I have seen people sleep with their eyes wide open and it always scares me. Was he asleep? At that moment hodoshe sat on his forehead, danced a bit, preened its wings and then settled. I hated these blue-flies because they are always associated with death. It walked gingerly down, around his left eye and then turned towards his nose. It jumped onto his lower lip and preened itself again. Something must have startled it because it jumped and flew towards me. It sat on my knee and without thinking I slapped at it and squashed it. Jola started and looked at me with surprise. I wanted to apologise but thought better of it. It was just a fly after all.

"Dlangamandla, money can make you blind to the truth. When things turn sour money cannot bail you out. Sometimes you get scarred for life, mhlobo wam. That is the situation I find myself in at the moment. I have money but it cannot help me. My dreams – all of them – have been dashed. I had prayed to God for wisdom and a good life. He gave those to me. I prayed that He give me a son. He answered that too. But by the time He gave me a son I had already made the worst mistake of my life. Now I have lost everything."

He covered his eyes with his trembling hands and let his tears fall.

A long time passed before he began speaking again, "While I was away from home, Dlangamandla, I spent a lot of time in hotels and guest houses. I lived like a king. But then I became sick. I did not know what it was but I thought it would soon pass. I secretly went to specialists and amagqirha to find a cure, but I was not getting any better. I lost a lot of weight and I could not come back here in that state. I was ashamed. At one point my wife called to say I should come home urgently. She said it was about my son, my unborn child."

He choked and I waited until he recovered.

"Although she did not say what was wrong, I feared for the worst. I was afraid of knowing, so I did not come back. One of the men who had come back to the village told me about my wife's condition. He said she had cut herself off from everyone and everything. My house was disintegrating and my daughters were not well looked after. I knew then that I would have to pluck up courage and come back."

He swallowed hard. I could tell that he had come to the heart of the matter. I was torn. On the one hand I wanted to help my friend, while on the other I did not want to know what was troubling him so deeply. I always tell myself that bad news is like cancer. Once you hear it, it gets to you and devours you. Should I tell him to go to his family and not bother other people with his troubles? Why should it be me who should carry his cross?

I became embarrassed when he looked at me with eyes full of hurt and sadness. I had to say something to fill the space that was widening between us. I had a strange feeling that I was fast losing my friend. In my mind's eye I could see him falling into a deep, dark hole.

"Jolinkomo, you know I will never desert you, no matter how dark your tale is. We have stood up for each other before, I do not see why that would change. Trust and believe in me and your burden will be lighter."

I said this without any conviction.

"Jola, no matter what problem you have, you must share it with people you love and trust, people who will stand by you through thick and thin. I think I qualify to be one of those," I said, trying to be bolder. "Qualify" sounded the right word to use. I was proud of the way I was handling the situation.

"Unyanisile ntanga, that is true my friend," Jola replied. "But I have seen people turning their backs on their friends. I do not blame them. Sometimes people have problems of their own. They cannot cope with more. But there are just too many taboos in our society. It scares me. Family members do not talk about certain things because that goes against culture. But the truth is the more we remain silent the more we will perish. Dlangamandla, in my case I am not blaming ignorance, instead I think I have been a bit arrogant. Because I had money to throw around I thought I could solve all of my problems. When I could not get a son I became selfish. Although I still loved and cared for my wife, I began to cheat on her."

He said the word "cheat" with disgust.

"I must be honest with you," he continued, "I did not cheat in order to get a son. I cheated because I had power, power to have any woman I fancied. Conquering women became my passion, second only to my business. I didn't care how much I spent on them, I was making more than I was wasting. When you live a life like that, you often pay the price. Three weeks ago a woman I had stayed with for a while in Matatiele called me. She told me that she was dying of AIDS."

I knew then I had to do or say something. But what?

Then he said, "Ntanga, my son is infected too," and I knew I had to act. I offered him my hand and we stood up and walked slowly together. At first I did not know where we were going and I did not care. Then I realised we were heading towards the river. The river we swam in as children, the river where we washed away imbola as young initiates, the river whose water has sustained the whole village for decades. When we reached the bank, we removed our shoes and waded into the water. A few paces downstream the small boys and girls of our village were playing in the water. As I looked around I thought, life is so beautiful and for it to flow like this river we have to act today. We watched the children in silence. There was a smell of rain in the air.

Mthuthuzeli Isaac Skosana

Just a Child

Dedicated to Baby Tshepang

I'm just a child
I'm just a little girl
I'm just a baby girl waiting
waiting to be picked up
by the hands of a father
or uncle
or neighbour

I'm just a little daughter
The one you cherished with a name
I'm your little daughter

I'm just a neighbour's child
The one you bought gifts for
The child you said you would look after

I'm just a child
not prescribed as a cure
I'm not your HIV medication
even my scream could not stop you
your ears are my witness
I'm just a child.

Jenny Robson and Nomthandazo Zondo

Baba's Gifts

MaNdlovu looks about the yard and yes, it is clean. Everything is in its place for her husband's homecoming from the mines. Her children are clean too, well scrubbed. Dlamini will be pleased to find such good order when he arrives.

But still MaNdlovu cannot relax. She feels her heart beating too fast. On her back, the baby is restless, sensing her nervousness. How will she say the words she must speak to her husband?

Her son, Vukile, comes back from checking the cattle. The sight of him gives her heart a little peace. Her first-born! So strong and so handsome at twelve years in his smart white shirt.

He says, "Ma, what is it my father will bring me from the city? What do you think Baba's gift for me will be?"

MaNdlovu enjoys teasing her son.

"Maybe it will be a box of matches, my Vukile? Yes, that will be a fine gift! A nice box full of matches for you!"

Teasing Vukile makes her feel a little less nervous.

"No, no, Ma!" Vukile wails. "Not a box of matches. I want a football! Will Baba bring me a football, do you think?"

MaNdlovu feels her fierce love for her son wash through her and make her brave. And she will need to be brave when her husband comes. For the sake of her family, for Vukile and little Ntombi and the baby, she must have courage. There are things she has to say. She has been saying the words over and over in her mind. But what if the words are wrong? What if they only make Dlamini angry? He is a man quick to anger. And sometimes she is afraid of him, especially when he has just returned from the city, smelling of strange city smells.

The sun is low beside the hill and over her tidy yard. Soon it will be time for the bus to arrive. So MaNdlovu walks the dusty downhill path with her baby sleeping on her back. Should she speak to her husband as soon as he is off the bus? Maybe it will be best to get the words out right at the start.

The bus arrives after an hour's waiting. MaNdlovu watches her husband alight. He looks like a stranger in his city clothes after all the months he has been gone. She forgets when she is alone how tall and strong Dlamini is. She greets him, smiling shyly to show she is joyful that he has returned. Because the people in the bus are staring down at her, watching.

Dlamini hands her a packet.

"See, MaNdlovu, I have brought chicken pieces for our supper."

She thanks him for the gift. She lifts his heavy box of belongings onto her head. He is still talking as he strides ahead of her, as the bus rattles off in a cloud of evening dust.

"How have the rains been, my wife? And my mother? Is she well? Did you take her to the clinic for her chest?"

And now? Is this a good time to speak, while they are still some distance from home and alone on the path? MaNdlovu takes a deep breath and addresses her husband's broad back.

"Dlamini, my husband, I have serious things to ask you. Will you listen well before you answer me?"

But her husband has already seen his friends. He is calling out loud greetings to them and they call back to him across the grass.

MaNdlovu accepts that now is not the right time. She continues on her way home with the box pressing down on her head and the baby tearful and restless against her back. She must make tea and prepare the chicken pieces. Meanwhile her husband has taken the path to his parents' home.

I will speak to him before supper then, she promises herself. That will be the right time. With the good smell of chicken cooking.

Back home, Vukile is still waiting, his friends gathered around him.

"Have you seen Baba's gift for me, Ma? Is it a football? Did you see it?"

MaNdlovu walks to their sleeping quarters with the fine corrugated roof. She sets the heavy box down, then looks around to make sure that all is well. Yes, the large bed is smooth under its white and blue cover. Such a lonely bed it has been all these months. And how many nights has she lain there unable to sleep wondering whether Dlamini is sleeping alone in the city or whether some city woman, wearing strong perfume, is lying beside him?

"You all know what your husbands do when they are away! Even if you keep silent, still you know very well!"

That is what Nurse Margaret said at the clinic in town. Nurse Margaret with her big face that makes her look almost like a man. Nurse Margaret who says the most scandalous things and speaks about the most private affairs there in the clinic waiting-room. Sometimes MaNdlovu wants to cover her ears with her hands. Sometimes she wants to run out of the clinic so she won't hear.

"Yes, ladies! The time is past when these things must be kept secret. For your own sakes, for the sakes of your children, we must speak these things out loud."

There is shouting in the yard now. Vukile is yelling at the top of his voice.

"A football! I have a football! Baba, this is the best gift! Ma, come and look!"

MaNdlovu leaves the sleeping quarters, and there is her fine son, smiling as if his face will come apart, kicking the ball now with his friends who have appeared from all directions. And there is little Ntombi, holding a doll up to the sky and talking to it as if it were alive.

Dlamini is smiling. He sees her and says, "I have a gift for you too."

He holds up a white blouse patterned with small red flowers. So white and so soft! MaNdlovu presses it against her face.

She sees that Dlamini is smiling down at her now, so she begins, "My husband, there is something we must speak about. It is for the children's sake and because you have been gone in the city so many months . . ."

But Dlamini interrupts her, "Why is the chicken not cooking yet? My parents will come soon, wanting to eat."

So MaNdlovu goes into the kitchen to prepare the food. Maybe it is better this way. She will wait till after supper, when Dlamini's parents are gone and the children are fast asleep. She will wait till she and Dlamini are alone together in the bedroom. That will be the best time. Yes, that is the time for husbands and wives to share important talk.

She cooks the chicken while Vukile plays with his football and Ntombi talks to her doll. And then Dlamini's parents arrive. His mother sits stroking the scarf her son has given her. His father taps tobacco into his pipe from the large yellow tin his son has brought him. MaNdlovu moves about quietly, serving tea and food, anxious to show that she is a capable, dutiful daughter-in-law.

She hears her mother-in-law say, "You chose well, my son. Your wife has been a good woman whilst you were away."

MaNdlovu is happy to hear this because Dlamini will be feeling kindly towards her, and then maybe he will listen to what she has to say. Maybe he will agree to her request.

There at the clinic waiting-room Nurse Margaret had said, "You will do this thing carefully. We all know how sensitive men are. We know how they are stuck in their ways and do not like new ideas. Especially new ideas from their wives."

Oh and it had been such a shock! Such a terrible shock and shame to see Nurse Margaret there, holding a wooden penis! Nurse Margaret, who wasn't even married! MaNdlovu had looked down at the floor, wishing she were somewhere else, anywhere else.

"And see, this is how the condom goes on," Nurse Margaret had said. She demonstrated with hands that were almost the size of a man's. "This is your protection, ladies. This is the way to stop city diseases coming into your homes. Especially the HIV virus that brings AIDS. It is all over the cities now. But with this condom, you can stop it from entering your home and making orphans of your children . . ."

MaNdlovu still feels faint when she remembers this. Though some of the women at the clinic laughed and joked about the size of Nurse Margaret's wooden penis, MaNdlovu could not laugh; the shame was too great.

The time has almost come. The night is dark now except for the round yellow moon. And her parents-in-law have left; proudly carrying the gifts their son has brought them. Dlamini himself is bathing in the warm water she prepared. And soon, soon, they will be together in the sleeping quarters. Together and alone in the darkness. But before that, she must speak.

What if it makes him angry? What if it makes him suspicious? She is afraid he will shout at her, "Why is my wife keeping such things in her bag? Is it because she is seeing other men while her husband is gone?"

MaNdlovu finds that her hands are shaking as she walks across to the sleeping quarters in the moonlit darkness. And there is Dlamini, already in bed beneath the blue-and-white cover. He looks so big lying there; his presence fills the whole room. She can feel the sweat lying on her face. She feels the word 'condom' sticking in her throat, almost choking her.

In the light of the lamp, her husband's eyes look dark and unfamiliar.

"Come to bed, wife," he says. "I have been away from you a long time."

With her hands still shaking, MaNdlovu opens the cupboard door, opens her clinic bag. She holds up a condom in its foil cover.

She says, "Please, Dlamini. It is for the sake of the children. It is because there are diseases in the city, diseases that kill. Nurse Margaret told us."

Is it anger in his eyes? Is he about to shout at her? The lamplight is blinding her and she cannot see her husband's face. It seems so much time passes before he answers. In her hand, the small square package is trembling wildly.

At last Dlamini replies with a laugh, "Nurse Margaret! Why do you listen to Nurse Margaret? She is an ugly woman who will never be married. So now she tries to destroy the marriages of other women. You throw that nonsense away, MaNdlovu. And then you join me here in bed."

And even though he is laughing, MaNdlovu knows she must do what he instructs, no matter what Nurse Margaret has explained. Dlamini has turned the lamp off now. In the darkness, without her small square package of protection, MaNdlovu gets into bed beside her husband. He still smells of the city, despite his bath.

Nape 'a Motana

Arise Afrika, Arise!

(for performance, accompanied by drums, xylophone and short pipe)

Yesterday Afrika ran red
with freedom fighters' sacrifice
Today, under the jaws of man-eater AIDS, red
as vicious viruses colonise black blood.

Afrika, stop AIDS!
He who pussyfoots towards
the lion of sexual temptation
must be armed with a burning spear!
Unarmed it shall be:
"Dust to dust . . ."
A funeral ox bleeds;
a dead man wears a casket;
survivors taste custard.

Today AIDS laughs
with reddened teeth,
coffins coughing death
tears tearing Afrikan cheeks.

But tomorrow on the monster's grave
with triumph-inflamed faces –
teeth egret-white,
songs pregnant with victory
we shall belch
when the shattered dream of
Patrice Lumumba and Mwalimu Nyerere
rises from ashes of AIDS!

Wake up Afrika, wake up!
Wisdom springs out of
a bleeding wound!

Arise Afrika, arise!
Out of the valley of skulls!
For AIDS viruses are no
spots of an Afrikan leopard!

Awake Afrika, awake!
Where is the man-child's mother
to grab an AIDS knife-edge
and break the dagger to pieces?

Arise Afrika, arise!
Lift up the shield of Shaka,
spear of Sekhukhune,
stick of Makana
and battle-axe of Nghunghunyani
to stop the lethal jaws of Kgolomodumo
death-wreaking monster –
from devouring the flowers
of your loins!

Arise Afrikan eagle, arise
out of the virus valley
your giant wings
higher than Mount Kenya,
glittering as Kwame Nkrumah's
ultra-bright star!
Arise Afrika, arise!

Unite Afrika, unite!
One hand, one stone
crushing the diabolical head of the serpent!
Re tla fenya ngokunqoba ngqo –
we shall completely destroy the enemy!
Arise Afrikan eagle, arise!

Puseletso Mompei

I Hate to Disappoint You

I hate to disappoint you, but the truth is, since I've found out I carry the virus, I haven't changed too drastically. I haven't sunk into a web of confusion, or wallowed in a bucket of tears. That has never been my style. Not about anything, certainly not about this. I learned at a young age that life will throw me storms, and this is just like any challenge. I know I will survive.

I know you might be disappointed by my lack of drama, that I never wanted to attempt suicide, or that my despair did not keep me locked in my flat for days. Or that I still put on lipstick and walk with my head held high as men whistle at me, or that my voice never quivers when I speak to my demanding boss. You may be disappointed to know that my hair still grows as thick as it ever did, that I still think I deserve success and that I'm still as forceful as I was. Basically, I'm not the pity-pot you'd associate with being a typical HIV victim.

Since the first cases of HIV/AIDS were recorded, people living with the virus were enveloped in a casing of secrecy and sympathy like you wouldn't believe. It's almost like you gain the status of martyr in some people's eyes. Yes, there are those who hate you and refuse your touch, but there are those who think you are about to fall dead on your feet any second, and treat you like a helpless frail thing. "Good" people who hold no prejudices want to create a fairy tale of "people like you and I, who should be treated with sensitivity". Sensitive, politically correct journalists have made careers out of soppy stories. They have played a huge role in promoting this permeating myth, that all HIV carriers are angels who have been hit by an undeserved dose of this virus. I refuse to embrace this pervading thought. Look at this article in my hand. It says:

> *Victims of HIV need us to touch them, not be afraid. We should not forget that their days are numbered and that every hurtful slur cuts to the core of their being . . .*

I cannot embrace that flowery prose, that's why I'm fundamentally the same woman I was and haven't turned into this caricature. We all deserve kindness and consideration, don't undermine my self-worth by exaggerating this need while I'm still young and vibrant.

If you thought I was going to tell you another heart-rending, sad story about a woman who never saw it coming, you can call in someone else to feed you a sob story. I was a '90s teenager, I knew HIV was out there. I knew that it could happen to me. If you realistically look at the situation in my country, you'll see that chances are someone you know will be HIV positive. And it just turned out that 'person' was me. To say I never saw it coming would be taking denial to a high degree. Like most people I was going on the assumption that HIV was not a real possibility, just like losing a job you love. You think "God wouldn't dish that out to me . . ." But I still knew that it could happen to me. I'm really surprised by stories of women who claim they never, ever thought they could be HIV positive. Who feel the ground being sucked from beneath them, who seem to think their naivety would be an immunising factor. To anyone carrying this idea in their head, I say look at the statistics, they spell out everyone's chances pretty clearly.

I hate to disappoint you by looking as good as I do. This is not how an HIV-positive person is supposed to look. But therein lies the quandary. How are we supposed to look? Are we supposed to suddenly have sunken eyes, dry lips, hollow cheeks and bent, stooping shoulders? That change in appearance doesn't happen overnight, nor is it my destiny. I could be knocked over by a careless driver tomorrow, still as healthy as I was years ago. Despite the reality that there are millions of HIV carriers running corporations, commanding flourishing businesses, teaching children in schools and flying planes, we are still fixated by the image of a solitary dying man who was filmed lying on a hard hospital bed. His body is ravaged by the disease, and you can count every rib beneath his leathery skin. While this is a compelling image, it is annoyingly one-dimensional.

I hope you're not too put off by my still-rich voice, and wonder when I will realise that I'm dying and bring an end to all this bravado. But we all display bravado in tough situations, why should I stop now that I'm HIV positive?

I hate to disappoint you with my apparent arrogance. Yes I'm facing a serious disease, but so are people carrying undetected brain tumours. Yet they are expected to feel as though they are entitled to a degree of dignity I don't deserve. By wanting me to say I feel deflated, defeated and finished, you want me to say I'm ready to take my last breath any second now. That is simply not true about me, or millions of HIV-positive people out there.

As I said, I'm fundamentally the same woman. But not exactly. There are a few things I struggle with, which is why I felt the need to talk to you. I met this man, his name is . . . well let's just call him T. I was attending a board meeting, standing in for my boss. This tall commanding figure walked in, but I decided that he was probably used to women falling all over him and that I wouldn't look at him for a second more than I needed to. But he turned out to be a really nice, down to earth man, and that is what I liked about him. Despite my cold reception he was so easy-going and comfortable in his skin that I soon forgot I was supposed to be keeping him at arm's length. We became friends, and in the month we've known each other we have had daily chats and had a meal together.

So then we get to the point of my dilemma: having a relationship with a man when you're HIV positive. I keep thinking to myself I'm fretting too much, that after he finds out my status he'll reject me and I won't have to worry about being a health risk to him. But more than being rejected I worry about having to face this reality with another person. What if he decides he can deal with my status and wants to be with me despite everything? See, I've been handling this thing single-handedly, quietly taking care of my health, going to gym, eating right, reading up on HIV, vaccines, T-cells, viral loads and all sorts of things. It has been *my* problem and I have had the freedom to handle it the way I want to. On some days I just don't want to think about it at all, so I don't. If I let another person in on my status that would force me to deal with his reactions, his concerns and whatever emotions he is grappling with. If I let him know I am HIV positive I'll have to face his questions, even on days when I don't want to. I'll have to hold in my coughs when I have flu so he doesn't get scared. I'll have to make sure I never touch his razor blades in case I get my blood onto his blades. I'll have to tell him when I progress from being HIV positive to having full-blown AIDS. Basically, this is the part I'm struggling with when it comes to this whole HIV thing.

So now I'm sitting here wondering if I will keep spending time with him or if I should end it now. The thing that worries me is that this situation will follow me around for the rest of my life. Suppose I break things off with T before they get serious, what about the next man who likes me, and the one after that? That is the biggest challenge I think I have faced so far concerning my status.

My fighting instinct is as sharp as ever, but I'm still realistic about my status. Just because I refuse to have it define me doesn't mean I forget that I'm living with HIV. I'm still determined to be filthy rich, to travel the world, just as I'm determined to live as positively with HIV as I can.

I hope I didn't disappoint you with my lack of remorse, or tears. I hope you start to realise that beautiful women carry HIV as well, that we still swing our hips as we walk into parties, that we are socialites and trend-setters. That we grapple with issues in our relationships, but can maintain our strength at the same time. I hope you expand your definition of HIV positive and stop thinking of us as skinny prostitutes who live in shacks, using candles for light. We are more than that. I hate to think this truth might have disappointed you in any way.

Nasabanji E. Phiri

Not at All!

My grandmother, you seem puzzled,
You liken it to influenza,
Influenza was better,
It came and went.

You say, how come, my daughter?
Not at all, my granny,
It is not like the great drought,
For the drought was and is no more.

What then is it like, my daughter?
Is it like the smallpox, which took
Your grandfather in his youthful days?
Not at all, grandmother,
Smallpox is no more.

Listen old one, this one is like a fire
That burns intently in the depths of hell,
Yes, burning slowly with its heat
Burning the cursed in its chambers.

It is like a thorn that pricks continuously,
Piercing the flesh, and not regressing.

It is like the mamba,
Whose deathly strike
Paralyses the heart instantly.

Yes – old one, it is called AIDS,
Look at your grandchildren,
Where are their mothers?
The mamba struck once
Without sympathy,
Leaving great sorrow behind it.

Tell the world, wise grandmother
That it is not at all like yesteryear
When the medicine man could rush to the rescue.
It is AIDS, grandmother.
Not like any of the other sicknesses,
Not at all.

——◆——

Mbonisi Zikhali

N.O. C.U.R.E (No One Can Understand Real Endurance)

Who waits for the sun to rise
At the stroke of midnight?

Who waits for the bread to bake
Before he sets out to harvest the wheat?

Who waits for tomorrow
When he missed today?

Who endures a question
That has no answer?

It is surely the disease
That has no cure.

Tracey Farren

The Death of a Queen

Cecelia came to the door in an old bathrobe, baby blue with wild loose threads. Beneath it she wore a Beacon Sweets T-shirt and a towel twisted into a nappy.

"I can't come to work." She put a hand to her stomach and looked away while she gathered her breath. When she spoke again her voice was strong, like a bold note at the end of a song: "I am feeling weak."

Her baby lay amongst the scrambled blankets, staring at the low roof and pulling his mouth into an exploratory "o".

"He's been crying all night . . . cry, cry, cry."

She sat down slowly and put shivering hands to her eyes.

"I just need some days. Next week I will be better."

She passed her matric a month before the baby came. It had taken two years of going straight from work to night school where she warred with the English terms. She laughed helplessly in the class, but later on in her shack she wrestled them into her head until her eyes surrendered to the dim candlelight. She was up way before the sun, ironing her skirt and combing the knots from her hair. Once she had her matric and her baby, she said, she would think again. She would move closer to town and her boyfriend could support her for a while – he had that painting job at the docks. When the baby was older she would get a job in a shop. She would have a certificate to show. "Geography" and "Business Management," she laughed at herself, her sharp teeth making neat shapes in her dark velvet face.

"Oooh hoo!" she sang, "I don't know how I'm going to do it!"

But when Cecelia passed her exams, she had seemed unsurprised.

"I am lucky," she said gravely. She had God to thank because the lump in her neck that had appeared last year had receded to almost nothing. She had prayed hard for it to go away and the sangoma had given her cream. To hide the swelling she'd had nice long extensions plaited into her hair – it had taken a whole day to do. By the time the extensions were out, her belly was just starting to grow. It was going to be a small baby, the doctor had said.

Her water broke late one Saturday night and she had not even finished washing when she knew that she could not keep it in. The pressure was like the earth closing in and her stomach felt like it was being sliced by a blade. Elizabeth from over the road came and sat with her. Still drunk from the evening, she buried Cecelia in blankets. Cecelia's groans pushed back the alcohol in Elizabeth's veins and stretched her eyes wide in sober fright.

"Push!" was all she could say. "Push!" she said, long after Cecelia had grown quiet. Cecelia reached down and pointed at the blankets between her thighs. "I am finished," she said with quiet dignity.

Elizabeth's hand found a warm, slippery form and held it up to show its furry head and tiny bent legs. She put an ear to the form and heard its whimper. "Oh God," she kept saying until they pulled into the hospital drive.

A nurse leaned in and screamed at her: "Can't you see he has the cord round his neck!"

Bulelani was peremptorily cut from his mother and Cecelia was left to her own sticky flesh. This was no place for bed baths and sweet cups of tea, only a stained basin and a paper cloth to dry with.

Bulelani was her angel, her precious love. He took the place of the baby boy she was forced to send to her mother when she was eighteen, and eased the sorrow of the miscarriage she'd had two years before. She couldn't bear to hear him cry and crooned to him in a high pitched tone, telling him that he was her life.

"He's a greedy boy." She held him up and shook him gently, still awed by his perfect face.

She laughed a deep laugh, a rich sound that came up from her womb and gathered love from her heart on the way. Her heart gave love like her breasts gave milk, endlessly and with grateful intention.

She breastfed until she got sick.

"One week," she repeated, "and then I'll be strong."

But the very next day she called me for help.

"I need to go to the doctor," she gasped, "I have pains in my feet."

"Aieee!" she cried as she swung her feet to the floor. She sat panting for a moment and her eyes moved heavily to mine.

"Please pass me my gown."

She shook horribly from the effort of dressing and getting into the car. As we turned into the sun-drenched street she smiled at the baby on her lap.

"Don't worry," she said, as if to us all. "Nobody is going to die."

The doctor could not find a cause for her breathlessness or the stabbing pain in her feet. She referred Cecelia to a government hospital for tests. Cecelia sat waiting on a hard wooden bench for two hours, using the last of her strength to clamp her handbag to her side and stop her baby from rolling onto the floor. The nurses came just before she lost consciousness and laid her on a bed. By the time I arrived, she had fought herself awake again in response to the baby's cries.

"Take him," she gasped. "I just need one night."

They treated her for TB, pelvic infection and an ulcerated throat. Her weight dropped as if burnt off her frame and by the end of the week her eyes were huge and bright and already grieving. I lay the child across her lap and she smiled a pretty, white smile.

"My baby," she whispered, but could not even move a hand to touch his tranquil body.

When I lifted him off her, she lowered her eyes.

They discharged her the next day and I found her swaying on her thin legs, determinedly packing a bag. She put on some lip balm and checked for her handbag again. As she tied a careful double knot in a Pick 'n Pay bag, a ragged beam of light leaked into the room, lighting her regal cheekbones and her calloused, careful hands.

I mumbled to her waiting boyfriend, "She must have been a queen in another life."

He nodded his head as if he knew what I had seen.

The nurses at the local clinic counselled her behind a closed door. She raged at them helplessly, her voice hard with despair, but came out subdued.

"I'm going home to my mother," she told us. "And I don't want those purple things," she said of her TB tablets, "they make me vomit all day. The baby will come with me. But I will send him back. There is no food for him in the Transkei."

Two days were all she asked. Two days to show her baby to her mother, to prove that her death would not be in vain. A life for a life, is what she wanted to say, and then he could return to Cape Town. Armed with soup for the journey and a gift of tea for her mother, Cecelia took a long-distance bus to her grave.

Tonye Stuurman

Everybody's Got It, Don't They?

So, what do you want to know? I get paid for sex. That's it. I have to work for a living, don't I?

One of my regulars asked me the other night, "So, Cookie, have you tested lately?"

I looked at him and said, "Honey, why didn't you ask me that two years ago when you started seeing me?"

You should have seen the shock on his face. I was surprised that he was surprised. What do these guys expect? They are the ones walking around with this sickness and then they pick up girls like me and infect us.

Hey, I'm not blaming anyone, but let's be real about this. These white guys in their fancy cars that cruise Main Road at night . . . they are the ones. And no, not only the fat, greasy guys. How do they call them? The yuppies.

The other night I was standing on my corner as usual. Dressed to kill – that's funny isn't it? In my jacket pocket I had my condoms and washcloth. Well anyway, a big blue BMW pulled up. The ou looked quite nervous. He stopped his shiny car, looked at me and slowly pulled away. I'm used to this. He'll come again, I thought to myself, they always do.

I was right. A few minutes later, the car was back. The automatic windows rolled down.

"Hi there," he said. He didn't look that bad – in his forties, dressed in a Polo shirt and Levi's jeans.

"So, what are you up to?" he said.

I am so sick of these rich guys being so prim and proper. Get on with it! We're not in a bar.

I put on my sexy smile. "What do you need, lovey? A blow or the full service? A blow is R40 and full service is R100. I promise you honey, you'll have a great time."

"Well, that's a lot."

These bastards have the money, but they never want to pay.

"Honey, that's the going rate, take it or leave it."

"OK, a blow-job then."

I signalled to my colleague on the other corner that I was leaving. You see, on the street we work as a team. If you don't have a pimp, you help each other. When one gets into a car, the other takes the registration number.

We parked around the corner. Nice leather seats, aircon, the works. Faces never matter to me. I am here to do a job, no more.

I had another job before, you know. I was a nurse. I worked bloody hard, but you know how much nurses earn? There was my mother, who suffered from arthritis and couldn't work, my sister still at primary school and no father. I was the only breadwinner. What was I supposed to do? Another nurse introduced me to this life. You'll be surprised at the number of pros on these streets. Well, I was doing very nicely with my two jobs – seven till seven at the hospital and a few hours after work on the street. Until one bitch saw me one night and ratted on me. That was the end of my nursing career. Now my mother can't move her fingers but I can afford to send her for the best treatment. And my sister, she's at varsity now. They don't know what I do for a living – they think I work at a coffee shop at night. So you see, I know all about AIDS and what is happening. I do read the newspapers, you know. I'm HIV positive and I try to protect myself as best I can. You can only ask the clients to wear a condom – you can't make them.

This is the way I make my living. I don't force anyone to cruise the streets looking for something they can live without.

Mbongisi Dyantyi

The Homecoming

"I am afraid of having sex . . ."

There was total immobility in the hall. It seemed that even the air stopped moving.

"Mmpf!" The sound echoed in the silence that followed Sammy's confession. It was full of Nomalizo Gxeka's ridicule and tightly controlled malice.

"Nomalizo?"

The question was soft, but Nozizwe Diliwa's voice was unmistakably authoritative. She was the founder and director of Ukuthetha Isisombululo. She would be the first to admit that she was founder and director of not very much. Ukuthetha Isisombululo was, for the time being, nothing more than a space created by her for people to speak about their problems. They had no offices, no funds and only one failed attempt at a Bachelor of Arts degree between them, hers. Though the hall, the only one in the township, was given to them to use free of charge, it was not ideal. It was too big for her group of eight, so it always looked empty when they met. It faced south and was endlessly cold. But worst of all, there was no privacy. Even the most illiterate of the township knew what "community hall" meant and were quick to tell her that the hall was not hers alone.

"We disagree. We voice different opinions. But we also listen and never judge," Nozizwe said, surveying her group.

She had come to know them well over the five months in which she had laboured to make this support group a reality. They sat in a circle, inspired by the legend of King Arthur and the Round Table. To her right sat the twins Mpho and Sipho. They shared almost everything. That was the reason they belonged to this group. They had shared a girl who had given them the virus. They were from Kraaifontein but preferred to be known as coming from Cape Town.

"Near enough," Nozizwe always said to herself.

There were fears, unspoken, that their primary aim in sharing their stories was to draw attention to themselves. Nozizwe hoped not; HIV/AIDS was not a tool to be used to anyone's advantage.

Next to them sat Phindiwe Songeka. She practised "saam drink, saam slaap" – anyone, and there were many, who could afford to buy her drinks for a night earned himself the right to take her to bed. It did not matter to her who he was, what he did or where he came from. Her session had taken the longest. No one could understand why she had thrown her life away for a few lousy drinks. No one, that is, except Nozizwe, who had had an idea from the beginning. After endless questions from the group and evasive answers from Phindiwe, she had decided to intervene and speak to her privately. The poor girl's story of abuse and pain had made her cry. That night, alone in her shack, she had wept bitterly for childhood and innocence lost. She had cried for all children who were still suffering. But she had cried most for Phindiwe.

Then came Nomalizo Gxeka. She was nicknamed "the black beauty" – her pure black skin made her beauty extraordinary. While all around her there was a mad scramble to make brown skin a shade lighter, just a little whiter, her black beauty was unique. She knew it too. Her personal motto was, "Black *and* beautiful, baby, never black but beautiful." Her one consuming passion was to show the inferiority of men. She liked to think of herself as taking vengeance for all women. "She who controls the penis controls the man," she had often been heard to say. She changed men like she changed her underwear. Their tears and pain were like the nectar of the gods to her, sweet and unblemished. HIV/AIDS she viewed as a regrettable side effect of mixing with men.

"Please continue, Sammy," Nozizwe said encouragingly, bringing to an end her scrutiny of the group.

"I am a virgin. I've never had sex with a woman," Sammy said again, with a self-conscious smile. "I come from a strict family and my mother warned me early on in my life what happens to weak men who can't keep their things in their pants."

His dark skin revealed no blush but his demeanour made it clear that he wanted to fade into his chair. His eyes cast only furtive glances at the group and his hands were fluttering like restless butterflies. It was a good thing too. Otherwise he may have seen the laughter in the eyes of the twins. He may also have seen the hunger in Nomalizo's gaze or the steely-eyed glance of Nozizwe as she quelled any remarks. Met by silence rather than the laughter and incredulous exclamations that usually followed this announcement of his, Sammy continued, shielded by his inexperience.

"My father left us when I was very young. All my life I vowed never to have anything to do with women. All women are dirty and are out to reduce men to a piece of bread. But I feel things," he said hesitantly, "things that make me feel guilty, and angry. Sometimes I dream things, things that

117

make me wake up sticky wet down there," and he shyly pointed to his crotch. "But always I think about my father."

This time the silence was crowded, full of the broken pieces of the bruised lives in the hall.

"My father is a real African man," said Sindiswa Mantyi.

Sindiswa's real name was Sindiso Mantyi. But he had long ago forsaken his birth identity. Sindiso had always loved being a girl. Dolls and not toy cars had interested him. Later he had found high heels fascinating and lace panties more to his style. Underpants, he had found, were too coarse for his liking. But his father was a "real man". A sour smell, a blue eye from a street fight and soccer was his idea of what a good boy should be. When Sindiso had had enough of pretending he had moved out of his home and became Sindiswa. His father was furious. Shortly after declaring himself a woman trapped in a man's body, Sindiswa was gang-raped.

"Feel what being a woman is all about, moffie!" his rapists had screamed at him, taking turns, forcefully entering his anus over and over again.

He refused to believe the rumour that his father had hired the rapists. For if he had, then he had effectively sentenced Sindiswa to a sure death. Sindiswa was now a silent and withdrawn person. In the group he was content to just sit and listen to the others asking awkward questions and giving unsolicited advice. But this time he felt compelled to speak.

"An African man," he said again, more softly than before and with a mixture of pain and pride in his voice. "You should have seen him when I came back from the bush. Tall, proud, confident that the traditions of his people had cured me."

For a moment it appeared that he would say more but then he must have remembered where he was, for he looked quickly around, cast his eyes down and mumbled an apology.

Nozizwe let it pass. It might have been because Sindiswa rarely spoke unless begged to, and even then he was embarrassed afterwards.

"My father is nothing but a ghost," said Sammy vehemently, showing some spark for the first time since they'd known him. "I used to remember his smell, the smell of smoke and the blood of sacrifices. But now I would not even spit on him should I pass him burning to death. I hate him and hope I never see him in my life, ever. I will probably never see him again," he ended, as if to himself.

"Why, Sammy?" Nozizwe asked.

"That piece of flesh hanging between his legs," interjected Nomalizo vehemently. There was nothing but a fierce look in her eyes now, but if it was directed towards Sammy not even she knew.

"Don't mind the tigress here, boy, she just needs a real man to tame her," said Mpho. Next to himself and his twin he loved nothing better than baiting the black beauty. She had shown nothing but contempt for him. The gaze she levelled at him was cold enough to freeze a lake.

Nozizwe looked at her watch. There was no more time.

As the group walked out she held up a hand to detain a young couple.

"Why were you both so silent today, Mr and Mrs Tomose?" she asked jokingly, but there was more than a little fear in her heart. The virus caused destruction wherever it went. Even the institution sanctioned by God was under severe attack.

Mrs Tomose opened her mouth to speak.

"Don't start, Nozukile," the man growled. Calling his wife by her marriage name was always a bad sign. It was unfailingly a bid to assert his dominance.

"Don't tell me you still refuse to sleep with your wife, Mandla," said Nozizwe, "I thought we sorted that out when you told your story?"

"We did, but what man can lightly forget the infidelity of his wife?" Mandla asked, looking over both their heads. "Especially if it brought death into the house."

It was on the tip of her tongue to ask him about his many infidelities, to ask about the meaning of marriage and forgiveness. But Nozizwe sensed that he was spoiling for a fight and the last thing she wanted was to fuel his anger.

"Remember Mandela, Mandla, who taught us the real meaning of manhood, who showed us that reconciliation, not fighting, is the true greatness of our nation," she said instead, hoping that an appeal to a real-life hero might bring him to his senses.

He looked at her for a moment, looked at his wife and then with a curt "Let's go" turned on his heels and left, with Nozukile hurrying to catch up with him.

"At least he did not beat us both up," Nozizwe mumbled, consoling herself and hoping for the best. Then she walked out of the hall and into the faded grey of dusk.

The noise of the township changed with the turn of day. There was the oppressive silence in the early hours of dawn, when only restless spirits and a few unfortunate souls that had to start work early walked the streets. Then at a more acceptable hour the gradual awakening whispers grew to a peace-shattering crescendo that only ended when the children were safely in their classrooms and their parents reluctantly at work. Then followed a lazy murmur generated by the old, the very young and the unemployed.

119

This was soon carelessly shattered by the energetic restlessness of school-children released from their bondage. Nozizwe loved the time when the workers returned from the city. She had dubbed it the homecoming. It was the most frenzied hour. There was the incessant hooting of the taxi horns, the screech of tyres and the indignant shouts of motorists and pedestrians. This was the time in which everyone made his or her way home. There was a background noise like the drone of a thousand bees.

Nozizwe could still hear the sounds of the day humming around her as the darkness of her shack swallowed her up. The voices of Phindiwe, Sammy, Nomalizo, Sindiswa, the twins. Mr and Mrs Tomose.

For me, reflected Nozizwe, there will be no rest tonight.

Felix Mnthali

Our Diseased World

(excerpted from the longer poem "Return Jembemziro")

Our world
is not all that rosy, grandpa:
we are dying like flies
from diseases you never heard of or saw
in your time
diseases that float in the firmament
in acts of affection and acts of begetting;
in acts of growing up and in simply
getting old and perhaps living well!

You must see the pain, grandfather,
the pain of looking at skeletons
that were once your friends and your kinsmen
decomposing and falling apart
before your very eyes!

Beauty that might have
outshone the sun is so swiftly, so completely,
and so suddenly disfigured.
You wait and you pray for wonders
knowing that the end has
like the beginning crept upon time
and crept upon the beginning
as suddenly as time began!

Some say all these diseases
were there in your day
only you never thought
they were something to be worried about
since there would always be a cure at hand;
some even say
you had herbs for such ills
and that we in our foolishness
have lost them all and even sold
quite a few
for a bag of salt and a sack of sugar!

Angifi Proctor Dladla

She Became the Mother Again
(Wa Phenduka Umdlezane Futhi)

She became the mother again
to her daughter of 47 –
Changing nappies;
washing her,
force-feeding her . . .
And, Lord, she sighed a lot
on that sleeping mat!
She became the mother again
to that city misfit.

In they came with gods and wisdom;
out they came touched, drained and haunted.

She became the mother again
to her grandson of 23 –
Changing nappies;
washing him,
force-feeding him . . .
And, Lord, she cried a lot
on that sleeping mat!
She became the mother again
to that prison drop-out.

In they came with gods and wisdom;
out they came bent, tired and wounded.

She loved them all;
yet they left her alone
with the cause
of their deaths – and,
without a mother . . .

This woman of 1920.

Sindiwe Magona

Leave-taking

"God – I hate you!" Nontando screamed as the beautiful wreath of white roses left her hand to spiral delicately six feet down toward the coffin. "I hate you! Do you hear me? God, I don't love you. No more!" With the last word Nontando crumpled onto the ground in a whimpering heap. Heads turned and necks craned toward the source of that voice, of those terrible, terrifying words – words that stabbed the heavens.

A hush fell, leaving the scream to grow in the eerie silence. All eyes turned, hunting the figure now hunkered on the much-stepped-on sand at the head of the newly gutted grave.

At once, her husband, Thando, came to her aid. As did Lwazikazi, her sister. She stood propped between them as the grave filled till it lay gaily capped with fresh wreaths. Nontando was silent now, rivers of tears cascaded down her sunken cheeks.

The time was early afternoon, a little after two.

The day was a Saturday in December.

The place was the NY 5 Cemetery in Guguletu.

The sight was a sickeningly familiar one to the people of Guguletu: not just a funeral but the funeral of a young person. It was a sight familiar all over the country. For Nontando, the sight that day undid her. It was only too familiar to her family. They had walked this road before.

In the stunned silence a voice was heard remarking, "Yhoo! Lo mfazi akamoyiki uThixo? Good grief, does this woman not fear God?"

"Myeke, wena, uzibizel' amashwa. You let her be. She only invites misfortune for herself," replied another.

". . . and dust to dust," Reverend Seko intoned, sprinkling holy water onto the grave.

"Sun of my soul . . ." a man began the hymn which the mourners immediately took up. The Service for the Dead was over. All was over.

Still supported by Thando and Lwazikazi, Nontando stumbled away from the graveside towards the hearse. They almost had to drag her, her feet no longer responded to the commands from her brain. Her only daughter was dead, never to return.

In the hearse, now empty of the coffin, she sat slumped against Thando, that very emptiness stabbing her heart. Her eyes had become cold – black coals. Thando did not speak. The driver did not speak. Their youngest son, Vusumzi, and Lwazikazi, sitting behind them, did not speak. All was quiet as a grave.

Only her mind was screaming a storm.

Who would have thought? How many years was it now that this unseemly passing away of the young started and people in the bloom of youth began dying like flies? It was not long before all Guguletu noticed the peculiarity of it all. The strangeness of it. That more and more, the wrinkle-faced stood by the graves of full-cheeked youth. *Ought-to-be full-cheeked,* she hastily corrected herself, for, as she knew only too well, by the time death stole them, they were as gaunt as though they had lived for a hundred years and more.

When had it started, this plague?

Nontando remembered how she'd heard of it, for the very first time, in church – of all places. During the Passing of the Peace.

"Have you heard," Zandi, sitting next to her, whispered.

"Heard what?" she'd asked absentmindedly.

"The Zenanis have lost one of their daughters." She looked knowingly at Nontando, brows chasing her hairline. Seeing her blank look, Zandi continued, "Sesi sifo sabantwana. It is this disease of the children." And her face said she was not talking about the measles.

Sensing township gossip, umgosi, Nontando uncoiled her neck like a giraffe's. "Yinto ni ke leyo?" she asked, "And what is that?" She hated admitting she'd fallen behind in the vital township syllabus of mgosi.

It had all seemed such a far-away thing then. Remote. None of her business. Isifo sabantwanan. *Dear God!*

Then, of course, she didn't know anyone who was HIV positive, never mind suffering from full-blown AIDS. The disease was a distant rumour, something that belonged to strange people up in the northern parts of the country. Or Africans from elsewhere in the continent, Africans who were flooding into South Africa now that apartheid was a thing of the past. Oonozakuzaku abembath' umakoti – the marriage negotiators who shared the bridal mat – that is what amaXhosa called them. People who, because they had in some small way helped the liberation movements, staked a claim on the South African pie. Felt they were owed something. Had a right to invade the country, swamp it with their cheap goods, sow their strange diseases all over, deprive the people of the soil of jobs that were only now opening to them and for which they had had no training, no preparation under apartheid. All this before they'd had a chance to learn to negotiate their new-found freedom, to live meaningfully in the new democracy. She, for one, would not be the least bit surprised if, one day, it was found that these nozakuzaku had brought this AIDS thing to South Africa. No, she wouldn't.

The car came to a stop in front of the house – NY 74 No. 220. The medley she found there was a welcome reprieve to Nontando. The cooks were agitated. These were women who had stayed behind to watch the pots: gallons and gallons of umngqush' ongenambotyi – samp cooked without beans, a sign of mourning. This didn't make much sense, thought Nontando, since to accompany the samp was meat with vegetables. Why abstain from beans if one is to have potatoes, carrots, cabbage? To say nothing of dessert.

Not that anything made sense any more in these punishing days. Her sitting on this hard mattress on the floor of her bedroom, the chief mourner, the mother whose child has died. And this congregation of people in her house. Her furniture at the houses of neighbours. The big tent, standing for almost a month at the front of the house. *We have spent so much money hiring the damn thing, we could've bought our own by now.*

From the front room, a woman began singing, "Rock of Ages, Cleft for Me . . ." Nontando was sick and tired of the endless singing. And more so of what she knew was coming next – the preaching. The infernal goings on had given her a pounding headache.

All because –

But her mind couldn't wrap itself around the yawning gulf – the space between the embryo of thought and giving birth to it. So vast. The gulf had swallowed her child. Her eldest. The child owamophula ingono – who had broken her nipple, as amaXhosa say. And the only girl-child in her troop of five.

Gone.

No, she didn't want any food, thank you, she told her sister.

"You must eat, 'Ntando," Lwazikazi said. "You'll make yourself ill."

As though I care whether I live or die . . .

There are vultures out there, Lwazikazi said and put the plate, covered with the lid of a pot and wrapped in a new dish-cloth, on the upturned metal box that served as a table near where Nontando sat on her chief mourner's throne, the mattress on the floor.

Lwazikazi suspected her sister would not eat the food – then or later –

126

and she was concerned. Nothing had passed Nontando's lips for days. Lwazikazi was also worried about the vultures who went about hunting for funerals so they could inflate the stomachs that stuck to their backs, stomachs to whom food had became a stranger rarely seen. Poverty had stripped people of shame, and decorum was dead. Dead and buried.

Twenty-eight. Only twenty-eight. Dear God . . . pretty as a picture. Twenty-eight. Her whole life stretched before her.

Tears scuttled down, in and out the gorges and mounds Nontando's cheeks had become this year past. She snatched a tissue from the Gary Player box on the makeshift table. With absentminded impatience, as though her face were an unnecessary appendage, an irksome nuisance to be rid of, she scoured it with the tissue balled in her angry hand.

Just then the minister walked in. Nontando straightened the shawl carelessly slung over her shoulders and nervously patted the black iqhiya expertly wrapped around her head by her sister. But all the while, her eyes remained dead coals beneath the puffy lids.

In a flash, the scene at the graveside painted itself in her mind.

Was that reproach in Mfundisi's eyes? What did she care? What did this smooth-talking man know of her grief? She had meant every word she'd said.

Nontando had always had an iffy relationship with God but, to be on the safe side, had gone to church and more or less followed its teachings as well as the next person. Now she felt God had gone and betrayed her. Forsaken her. Made her the laughing stock of all Guguletu.

Meanwhile, Reverend Seko's kindly eyes rested dolefully on the bereaved mother. Any fool could see the poor woman's soul was in peril. The devil had her by the throat.

"Sister-in-Christ," the man of God said. His tone was subdued as befits a house of mourning. "I thought I should not leave without looking in to see how you are doing."

He was not going to make an issue of the outburst. This was a woman of influence in the church, the other parishioners listened to her. Besides, he could depend on her hefty contributions. And, the Lord knows, she had been given a heavy cross to bear.

"Enkosi, Mfundisi, thank you, Reverend," Nontando whispered back.

"Will we see you in . . ." Although this was a speech he'd said so often it was as familiar to him as drawing breath, he hesitated.

They agreed she would return to the routine her Sundays had known before the abomination. As soon as she was ready . . . felt better.

Never . . . She would never feel better . . . ever . . .

"Take your time," the minister said.

"Enkosi, Mfundisi." Nontando extended her right hand to clasp his proffered one, but it lay limply, dead in his soft and fleshy grasp.

"Remember, we hold you in our prayers," he said, briefly exposing his surprisingly even white teeth. "And come back to us soon."

"Ndakuzama. I'll try, Mfundisi."

Like hell. Where were you when I needed you? You and your wife and the whole congregation? Where were you when it could have mattered, made a difference? You and your accursed magosa?

Even as the man of God made his way out of the room, the horror that had visited her family suddenly swamped Nontando, engulfed her mind with the vicious cruelty of it all.

But who could have known? Who would have thought that truth could die? That meaning could stop having meaning, stop existing? Who could have known that all the truths we have always held dear could come to be so pitifully inadequate? That humanity could come to be chaff before a raging storm that the wise men forgot to predict? That the so-much-touted advances of learned men could be piss in the desert? And that inhumanity could be measured in fat bank accounts – profit and loss – in the face of such devastation. Who could have known that the heart of science is evil incarnate; greed sitting on plush velvet chairs, smoking fat cigars, quaffing vintage wine, diamonds on every finger?

An involuntary moan escaped her throat – low and raspy.

Who could have known that in my own family such auspicious beginnings could give birth to such terrible outcomes?

Nomathamsanqa – Mother of Good Fortune. Thami, for short, Tham-Tham for velvety moods. Her darling daughter.

Thami had met Mpumelelo at her best friend's wedding. Thami was maid-of-honour and Mpumelelo the best man. Hard on the heels of that wedding came their whirlwind courtship. All in style. All in good taste. Accompanied by the mirth and hilarity of young love.

Six months into the courtship, the young man announced his intentions. Nontando was overjoyed, her daughter had made a perfect match. Yes, at first she had been a little reluctant. Thami, at twenty-two, was a little young for marriage, she believed. But Thando reminded her she was eighteen when they'd married and a mother of two by the time she was Thami's age. Did she have regrets, he'd wanted to know. Thus reminded of her own youthful decision and the bliss it had brought her, her objections melted away and she gave her blessing to the couple. Thami was an attorney, recruited straight from university by one of the leading firms in Cape Town, and Mpumelelo was an oncologist at Groote Schuur Hospital. Nontando believed happiness was guaranteed for the young couple.

The wedding was a grand affair that people in Guguletu still talked about, more than five years later. There were horse-drawn carriages, a fleet of white Mercedes-Benzes, food to feed Shaka's armies. The bridal gear earned her daughter the pet name 'Dee', as amaXhosa call the late Princess Diana.

But it was not long before problems sprouted and Thami was threatening divorce – on grounds of infidelity. Mpumelelo's eye was a busy one and it roved often, leading the owner to graze forbidden pastures.

Nontando choked as she remembered her words to her daughter.

"Nyamezela, ntombi yam. Ukwenda kukunyamezela. Patience, my daughter. To be the wife of a husband is to endure untold hardship."

Had she contributed to her daughter's death? Even inadvertently, was she an accessory to Thami's murder?

No two ways about it, Mpumelelo had killed her daughter. Nontando was as convinced of that truth as she was of her name. But the gnawing, niggling question remained: could Thami have escaped her fate had she, her mother, not persuaded her to stick with it? Stick with her marriage . . . her husband, the murderer?

Singafana nje siyiteketisa, siyihlonipha, bubugebenga, qha ke. Doesn't matter what euphemisms we use, this is nothing but murder, pure and simple. Finish en klaar. What kind of a mother was she who couldn't protect her children from the ruthless chopper?

A mother with pride in her heart, pride that blinds her to unsavoury truth.

Nontando had not wanted to hear of problems in Thami's marriage. She had told her daughter, the marriage was still new. Give it time. Besides, how many married women in the townships could honestly say their husbands had never strayed? Not once . . .

To make her point, knowing the answer, she'd asked Thami, "Have you caught him with a woman?" And thought she'd bought her daughter time. Time to grow into wifehood, into understanding the rigours of marriage. She was perfectly aware she had bought herself time. Time to regroup.

She was still reeling from the wounding news of Luthando's illness. Why, they had not even told Thami yet that her brother was HIV positive. None of the other children knew. He had told his parents and only the three of them carried the bitter knowledge in their mouths like some rare delicacy too precious to squander in a gulp. What they were savouring was fear. Naked fear. Liberally laced with bewilderment. And with shame.

What was a man's roving eye to her son's imminent death? She was sure Thami would understand one day. *Dry rot!* What she had done was put down a deposit on her daughter's casket – that's what.

"Ma! Guess what?" Thami's elation crackled through the line.

"How far gone?" Nontando asked, with a mother's intuition. No other news could have given such a lilt to Thami's voice.

"Seven weeks!" came the breathless reply.

Nontando made quick calculations. Aloud, she said, "I hope it's late August!" She herself was a Leo. It would be something, sharing a birthday with her first grandchild. Nontando's heart was full. AmaXhosa do say, uThixo uthwax'ephulula – God bludgeons but also massages, He softens the blows He deals us. They would have to hide Luthando's news a little longer. This was no time to stress Thami. She, and the precious life growing inside her, had to be protected at all costs. Let her get over the first trimester, at least.

She invited the expectant pair over for Sunday dinner. She didn't have to ask what she should cook for them. They both loved her umngqusho, cooked to a tender, juicy pulpiness; the creamy flesh of the beans pulverising and impregnating the corn. Why, Mpumelelo often left his meat untouched, gorging himself on umngqusho which neither he nor Thami had the patience or time to cook.

Thami's news brought a huge relief to Nontando. Now, with a baby on the way, the marriage would survive, just as she'd known it would. Sunday, she'd cook up a storm.

But Sunday never came. What did was the terrible telephone call. Till hell froze over, Nontando knew she'd never forget Thami's voice. A voice that was Thami's voice and yet not Thami's voice.

"What's happened, darling?" she asked, a snake slithering down her spine. "What is the matter?" she asked again, for in the numbing silence Thami had said nothing.

Then Nontando heard the silent tears washing down her baby's frightened face. Through the crackling telephone line, she could hear the sadness weighing down on Thami's heaving shoulders, drowning her very soul.

"Baby, I'm coming!" she whispered urgently and, not waiting for a response, corrected herself, "We're coming. Your father and I'll be there right away."

They were in Sea Point in twenty minutes flat. Thank God, they were going against traffic. On the way, they examined scenario after scenario, including that Thami and Mpumelelo had heard that Luthando had AIDS. It was possible, what with Mpumelelo being a doctor. But in the end Nontando came up with miscarriage as the worst possibility. They'd have been angry about Luthando – not desperate. And her daughter's voice had spelt utter desperation.

"What shall we say?" Thando asked as they parked near the entrance to Arthur's Seat Mansions, the block of flats where Thami and Mpumelelo lived. Thando, never one for many words, was sweating bullets. Nontando came up with just the right words to comfort a young couple whose first pregnancy would not come to fruition. They should not worry themselves, at least now they knew they could make a baby together, they were compatible that way. Also, the Old Ones say such events, sad as they are, must be seen as good omens. The baby may have been physically weak or malformed. This is nature's way of righting itself, the body's way of cleansing itself, umzimba uyazihlamba. Next time, she would tell them, the seed would germinate and grow to full term. Not to worry, all in due course . . .

But they had no way of escaping the inferno about to fall on their heads with the vengeance of the angry, unmerciful gods. Fall down on them as it was falling down on millions of other families throughout the country – indeed, throughout the world – with a reckless, crazy democracy: equal opportunity to the world's poorest. As it had already fallen down on them so that they had, without thinking, believed they had some kind of immunity. As though Luthando's illness had bought them precious, priceless inoculation.

Wrong.

Despair and a cold, fearful wrath married in Nontando's heart that day. That God could be so cruel, so unfeeling, so unforgiving. A terrible God.

A brief life. Aborted. Suctioned out of the cocoon of its mother's womb. Because there was no point to it. No point in carrying it to full term. No point giving birth to it. No point in expecting life and living. In fact, no point to anything at all.

Mpumelelo and Thami were unmoveable in their decision to terminate the pregnancy. At once. There was no point in prolonging it a day longer. That not only taxed Thami physically but unnecessarily, said her husband.

And you heard what the government's spokesman said, last week. *What shall we do with all these orphans?* Well, he and Thami certainly didn't want to leave any poor little orphan behind. What is more, it was their educated estimation that they had a good – no, better – chance of beating this thing if they were not distracted.

"And what would distract you?" asked the mother-in-law.

"Anything outside my wife and I."

"Any *thing*?"

"You know what I mean, Mama. Children. Family not paying attention to our wishes. It is our life . . ." he had the grace to taper off.

"But," at once, Nontando pounced, "we're here. We're family!"

Mpumelelo looked at her briefly then looked away.

That night, Nontando glimpsed a cruel truth: none of her other children were safe just because Luthando was ill. The lessons, unfortunately, were only beginning.

By the time they left Arthur's Seat Mansions, Nontando's eyes were prunes and her heart had become a cold stone. The death of hope. The birth of a terrible knowledge: *There is no god. If there is then he is a terrible, terrible god and I will have nothing more to do with him. Nothing, ever again. And I am not afraid of him for there is nothing he can do to me now that he has not already done. Let him do to me what he will.*

For the first time since Nontando had known of her son's illness, she went to bed without saying a prayer for him.

If she had believed she was suffering before, this new assault on her family jettisoned Nontando headlong into a private purgatory, for Thando chose to sit it out and have nothing to do with the pain and suffering swirling all around him.

But these children had lain under her very ribs; truly more flesh of her flesh and blood of her veins than anything of their father's. Thando could afford to distance himself from their suffering but she, through whose pain, sweat and blood they had come into this world, could not but feel each and every pang coursing through what was once so totally and utterly part of her.

Nontando wanted Thami to come and live with them in Guguletu so she could look after her. But her whole family was against it. Her husband felt she could not possibly cope with nursing two sick people. Hlumelo, their eldest son, said there was already enough gossip to go around the whole of

Guguletu with just one of them diagnosed with AIDS, and two was just too much. He'd have to move out and go and live somewhere else. Luvuyo came up with what was, in his mother's eyes, the most asinine reason of all. What about them? he asked. They had not done what these two must have done. Were they to be put at risk? He had exams coming. Why didn't everybody give him the same chance they'd all had so he could also finish high school and go to college? While Nontando understood his anxiety, she just didn't have the patience, time or inclination to deal with such crude selfishness right then.

Ten-year-old Vusumzi said the one sensible thing, "If it was me who was ill, I would love for Mama and all my brothers and my sister to look after me. Sis' Thami should come home, if she wants to."

Verily, out of the mouths of babes.

However, Thami's husband absolutely refused for her to be moved. What did they mean, *come home*? This was her home, next to her husband. Had they not vowed for better or for worse? Well, he wanted to nurse his wife himself, thank you very much. If it meant hiring a nurse, around the clock, then that is what he would do. But she was not moving. Nontando had to content herself with daily telephone calls and weekly visits from her daughter.

And Thami didn't seem to understand what all the fuss was about. There was no reason she could not go on with her life very much as she had done before. She was fine, she said. Besides, Luthando was too sick for their mother to be saddled with caring for her as well. And Nontando had to concede Thami looked fabulously healthy. While Thami displayed no symptoms of the illness, her mother did. She lost weight. Suffered bouts of sleeplessness, forgetfulness and irritability. At the sight of healthy-looking youngsters, she broke into tears. Her stomach was constantly running. Then one day, out of the blue, Luthando, who had contracted HIV through a girlfriend who had already died, asked her how Thami had been infected. Nontando realised that this was what had been plaguing her all along – *the how of it*.

If Thami had any idea, she was not saying. Nontando had her suspicions, though. Suspicions heightened by Mpumelelo's very caringness. But you cannot send a man to the gallows on mere suspicion. And it soon became quite clear there was a pact between husband and wife. The tight new bond between them, their silences in response to pointed questions, the sameness of their vocabulary – to listen to them was bizarre, surreal. The pact was strong; a wall surrounding them and keeping others out – out of this new and terrible thing that bound the two together and shut off the rest of the world. Bound them more than their marriage vows had ever done before.

And sometimes Nontando could see the sense in what they were doing. The world had gone quite mad and perhaps they were right to shut it out. What help had it been to her? Listen to the criminally ridiculous statements from the government! Poverty causes AIDS. Indeed! Then South Africa must be the poorest country on the face of the earth!

Nontando's anger was omnivorous; it devoured all: the church; the minister; his wife, leader of the Women's *Manyano*, the Mothers' Union; the wardens or *amagosa* and the congregation itself. This august gathering in its entirety failed to be of any help to her at all. It had offered not the slightest reprieve or consolation.

The Reverend's wife *asked her* what she thought the Manyano women could do.

"Why, what we always do when death visits any of our members' families," said Nontando. "I thought we could also start talking among ourselves about *esi sifo sabantwana* and perhaps warn those not yet infected."

"Dadewethu eNkosini, my sister in the Lord," replied Mrs Seko, wrinkling her nose and curling her lips in derision and exasperation. When she saw Nontando would not easily be sent away, she resorted to church canon. She would put the matter before *amagosa*, at the next vestry meeting.

Nontando knew full well that had Mfundisikazi wanted any of this to happen, she would have found a way to make it happen. Referring it to *amagosa* was killing it. She was not surprised when *amagosa* were up in arms that the request had been made at all.

"How can a true Christian suggest we talk dirty in church?" one wanted to know.

Nontando was incensed.

Talk dirty, indeed! How soon the African has forgotten what served them so well only yesterday. AmaXhosa had conveniently forgotten they had had sex education for the youth of the nation. Designated members of the extended family saw to it that girls and boys who had reached puberty had know-how that allowed them to satisfy the natural urges that were understood as such by our forebears. Do that without risking unwanted outcomes.

But then the white people came and killed all our ways of doing things, everything uniquely us. And, in our haste to be civilised, westernised and Christianised, how swiftly, how readily, we have turned our backs on our traditions, our ways of doing things.

Sadness laced Nontando's ire at the realisation of the nakedness of amaXhosa for she understood full well that a people without tradition are a people on the brink of perishing.

Mfundisi Seko was vague regarding any involvement or support the church could offer. Nontando decided the man of God was all talk and no action. She'd gone to him as a last resort only because Mfundisikazi and amagosa had let her down. Also, she'd heard, *she knew*, he had buried several young people who had died of AIDS-related diseases. These were children of parishioners. Surely, in the face of such devastation, such cataclysmic happenings, the church had a role to play? It could help halt the spread of this AIDS . . . surely?

"You did what?" Thando bellowed. He was furious that his wife had opened her big mouth and talked to the whole wide world about what was a private family matter.

At the unaccustomed explosion from her husband, Nontando shrank, suddenly afraid she may have overstepped her bounds. But surely she had every right to seek help for her children?

"Not the whole world, Father of Hlumelo, just our church."

"Those blabbermouths?" shouted Thando, eyes ablaze. "What will people say? And how could you besmirch Thami's name like this? She is a respectable member . . ."

"Excuse me," Nontando interrupted. "But this is not about Thami's character or behaviour. It is . . ."

But Thando cut her short.

"The trouble with you, Nontando, is you are selfish!"

Nontando flinched as though he had struck her a physical blow.

"Selfish?" she asked, astounded at the accusation, so unwarranted.

Here she was, minding Luthando, who wore nappies like a baby, feeding him because he was so weak he could hardly hold a spoon and, on top of that, cooking and cleaning and keeping house for all of them. And her own husband calls her selfish.

"Don't you see how you're going around begging for sympathy?" asked Thando. "What is that if it is not drawing attention to yourself? Taking it away from those who really deserve it, our children, both the sick as well as the others. They all need us."

"I'm sure I don't know what you're talking about," she threw at him. "You, who go to the shebeen every day, how can you accuse me of neglecting any of you?"

Thando changed his tune. Now he wanted to know if Nontando had asked Thami's permission before spreading the news of her illness.

"I'm not going to stand here and listen to . . ."

"Did she? Answer me, yes or no?"

"No, but . . ."

"There you are!" he crowed. "I hope you'll have the courage to tell her what you have done." He stopped, looked at her and shook his head before he continued. "Is it not enough the whole world knows of our disgrace, that Luthando has lo gawulayo, this chopper of a disease?"

"AIDS?"

"Stop that!" Thando screamed. "I don't want to hear that dirty word in this house."

"It lives here."

"It wouldn't, if the decision were up to me."

That stole Nontando's tongue. Silence. She could not believe what she'd just heard her husband say. She was at a loss for words.

And he, for once, wasn't. "Now people will think Thami, too, was loose. Just like this son of yours. What will the world think of us? Of how we raised our children? What are we to do in the face of such disgrace?"

Thando stormed out, no doubt to the shebeen, where of late he had taken to drinking hard liquor with other men who daily tried to drown their worries, their sorrows, their cares.

Thami was furious. She called her mother that same evening. On the way to Yuni's Shebeen, Thando had phoned his daughter from a phone booth and told her of her mother's actions. For weeks she wouldn't speak to her mother. This, of course, meant she didn't come to see her sick brother, only talked to him on the phone.

Aiding and abetting Thami's stay-away was her husband. Even when Nontando called to tell them Luthando was gravely ill, Mpumelelo refused to call Thami to the phone, saying her energy level was low and everything exhausted her. She was resting just then and he didn't want her worried unnecessarily.

Nontando resented every word from Mpumelelo's mouth but especially *unnecessarily*. How dare he?

Two weeks later, Luthando died.

Thami was inconsolable. She should have been told, she said. Everyone was making decisions for her as though she were brain-dead. It was insulting. Demeaning. When had she given up her rights to being human, that her family treated her like a piece of rock?

A week after her brother's death, Thami took a turn for the worse and had to be hospitalised. The first thing she did after she was admitted was ask for her mother.

Nontando rushed to Groote Schuur Hospital.

At once, she saw how the ravages of the disease had printed a map of suffering on Thami's pretty face. Her flesh clung to bone with a desperation that left her eyes seeming extra-large, buried deep in their hollow sockets. Her teeth had become spades. Pale, cold and papery to the touch were her hands and feet.

Don't do this to me, God. Please. What have I ever done to you that you should visit this curse on my head? Nontando prayed, forgetting she had abandoned God.

Thami was too ill to attend her brother's funeral.

In full mourning clothes, Nontando had one consolation: she could visit Thami every day now. Her eyes and those of Mpumelelo had become bitter enemies, spitting fire at each other. Whenever the two met, accusation and counter-accusation darted from eye to eye under flaring nostrils and furiously furrowed brows. One day, finding herself alone with her daughter, Nonthando thought it fit to straighten things out. For her peace of mind, if nothing else.

"How did this happen, Tham-Tham?"

At that use of the pet name of her girlhood, Thami's eyes reverted to an earlier form; they became, once more, the trusting, innocent eyes of yesterday. Briefly. All too soon, a veil fell over them and it was clear conflicting emotions were at play, fighting it out in Thami's heart.

She gave a wan smile and motioned for her mother to come closer, lean towards her – the better to hear what she had to say.

Her heart thudding as loud as a sangoma's drum, Nontando leaned over.

"Xola, wethu, Mama, please, be consoled!" she whispered. "Sekwenzekile. It is already so."

They had decided to be true to their love, their vows, and to apportion no blame, for, whichever way the disease had found its way into their bodies, neither one of them had wanted to die, neither had wanted the other dead, had wanted to kill the other.

"Hayi, ke, Ntombi yam, xa usitsho; mandiyekelele – well then, daughter of mine, if you say so; let me withdraw my question," Nontando said, defeated.

A knife twisted in her heart, even as she said those words. Mpumelelo had conned her little girl into becoming an accomplice to her own murder.

"Please, Mama, do not hurt yourself. We need you more than ever now."

Visibly calming herself Nontando said, "I'm listening."

"Tata and everybody else, they're all too scared to tell you."

Her stomach falling to her knees, Nontando said, "Tell me what?"

"I have been asked to tell you that another of my brothers . . ."

"No!" roared Nontando. "No! No! No!" she screamed as her daughter watched helplessly from her bed.

Nontando awoke from her sedation to the anxious eyes of her husband, who called the nurse on duty to let her know she had recovered. She still felt like a zombie as the car careered away from the hospital, homeward bound. She kept replaying recent events in her mind – over and over again. She cursed herself for a fool. Why had she not paid attention? Hlumelo's persistent colds. His loss of appetite. His loss of weight. Now, suddenly, it all added up. Why had she been so blind? But then, under all the recent stress, had they not all shown some of the same symptoms?

By the time he was diagnosed, Hlumelo had full-blown AIDS and was admitted to the same hospital as his sister. For the three weeks that both Thami and Hlumelo were at Groote Schuur, Nontando didn't know whether she was coming or going.

Mercifully, Thami rallied and was released from the hospital. But the reprieve was brief. She had not been home two weeks before it became obvious that she was losing the battle. But no more hospital for her, Thami decided.

Confronted with the unimaginable, Nontando found Mpumelelo's seeming good health offensive. Obscene. It was not right, she felt, that Tham-Tham should die while the known philanderer lived. Where was justice in that? Where, God? Although some said Mpumelelo had lost some weight and exhibited some of the symptoms associated with AIDS, Nontando saw none of that. In her eyes, he was the picture of good health – thriving. She saw only that he could walk where her darling had to be carried like a baby. He talked, she whispered. He gulped down enormous plates of food; Thami could only sip soup, clear soup at that. And could not feed herself that pitiful meal; even a teaspoon too heavy for her to lift.

Mpumelelo was at his wife's bedside day and night. He was as constant in his vigil as he had lacked constancy during the brief marriage. His frequent declarations of undying love lit stars in Thami's eyes. In death, she got what she had so craved in life. What had so eluded them: togetherness, oneness, belonging.

But Nontando saw the unfairness of it all. And hated this man – hated him more, the more her daughter adored him. One day, on her way to Sea Point, Nontando prayed to God. Yes, the same God against whom she fumed often and bitterly – she prayed to Him to punish Mpumelelo Zuba. To take him and let her daughter live. Or, if that was too much for God to handle, then take them both. But not to take her beautiful child while that skunk went on living.

God's ways, however, are not our ways, Nontando was reminded with blinding clarity the very day she let this uncharitable prayer slip past her unguarded lips.

"Mama," said Thami even before she'd returned her mother's greeting. "Vusumzi called. He said Hlumelo asked him to tell you to please hurry home."

At once alarm bells rang in Nothando's heart. But no, she told herself, it can't be that. Her son had seemed so much better when she left. This was one of his good days, the best he'd had in a long while. But then, what could it be? Why the summons?

Thami saw the questions racing through her mother's mind. Her heart bled for this woman whom she saw for the first time as a separate entity. A human being with all the frailty, strength, mystery and mysticism inherent in that definition. Separate from being Mama, whom one always and inevitably took for granted. She reached out – soul to soul.

She stretched out her arms to give her Mama a hug. Nontando fell into those outstretched arms as a baby to its mother.

"Oh, Mama," Thami said in a voice sure and strong. "I am so sorry . . . for your . . . suffering." She had to take frequent pauses between the words, but falter she did not, as she went on: "But, remember, time . . . is like a river. With bends, curves and jagged elbows. We cannot see those who are . . . around the bend but . . . we must . . . never . . . forget . . . they are there . . . they . . . are not . . . gone . . . We will never be apart."

Now Thami stopped. Halted. And, with love-lit eyes, beheld her mother as though seeing her anew. Caressing her. Admiring her with eyes clear as glass freshly washed. Then she continued, for Nontando had not interrupted, too choked with love to want to dilute the words coming from her daughter.

"Mama, you taught me, a long time ago," now Thami's words were not only sure and strong but continuous as though there was absolutely nothing the matter with her. As though she were holding a conversation under the most normal of circumstances, the words flowed, "that Spirit never dies. Love never dies. Therefore, we will never be apart."

The hug ended with wet cheeks and teary eyes. But these were tears of light, of joy, of love. Mother and daughter had found each other – on another plane. Thami begged her mother to please let her know . . . whatever the matter was. "Especially, if it's about my brother . . . I want to know. Please."

Nontando settled her daughter for her nap and left to hurry home. Yes, her steps were heavy, for the summons gave her dread. But she was uplifted, too, by her daughter's words.

Hlumelo was still alive when she got home. But only just.

"Mama!" he gasped, his face creased in a tender smile.

He was conscious to the end but could no longer speak. His brilliant eyes said a lot, though. He held his gaze steady, without fear or regret. A great solace to the family; especially to Nontando's grieving heart.

Hlumelo died late that night.

Early the next morning, Nontando and Thando drove to Sea Point.

"I know," said their daughter, as soon as she saw them come in. The parents were relieved at the calmness with which Thami accepted the news.

"She's at peace," the mother said on the way back and told her husband what Thami had said the previous day. Both drew comfort from her strength.

Again, Thami was not at the funeral, although this time she was not in hospital. The family felt she was too weak to attend. But she kept herself informed about the arrangements.

That Saturday, at one-thirty, she knew the funeral procession was leaving NY 74 No. 220 for the church. She could see it. See the people and the buses and the cars. She knew there were five buses: one for the rugby players alone; one for the teachers, for Hlumelo taught at one of the local high schools; another for the church people; and two for everyone else.

The funeral service at St Mary Magdalene Anglican Church, NY 2 would be from two to three-thirty. Then the procession to NY 5, to the cemetery.

Thami visualised it all. She was there with her mother and her father and her two brothers, Luvuyo and Vusumzi – Joy and Rebuild the Family. With what pride their parents had named them all, Thami smiled, going over the names of people she loved so much: Nomathamsanqa – Mother of Good Fortune; Hlumelo – New Sprig; Luthando – Love; Luvuyo and Vusumzi. The last two remained. Gone, Sprig and Love; and Good Fortune

140

barely hanging on. Perhaps . . . perhaps, after all, she had not been mis-named. Perhaps, her parents would still glean the good fortune that seemed so lacking, these days, in their lives. Perhaps, she'd be the last . . . the last to be taken to NY 5. Joy and Rebuild would survive.

"Ashes to ashes and . . ." intoned Reverend Seko in his baritone as he sprinkled the hungry grave with holy water. And Thami was there. She could see it all. Her family. The crowd. The church choir. She saw them all. Just as she could see her brother too. They were lowering the coffin into the grave now.

Right then, Thami slipped inside the coffin and there she was – lying by his side. Just as they used to when Mama made them take naps in the af-ternoon, when they were little.

They were close together, smiling at each other and looked on at the gathering assembled to pay homage to Hlumelo. They lay together, so very still, their eyes full of love as they beheld their parents and their two broth-ers. Poor Mama, helped to the car. Hlumelo and Thami sighed and looked away, full of compassion for their beloved mother.

On the way from the cemetery, the funeral party was met with the news of Thami's death. The family, it was decided, should not be told till they reached home. To the surprise of all, Nontando received the sad tidings in silence. But as the days grew and the silence continued so concern for her mounted. It was not normal, some said. Not natural, said others. But her silence lasted throughout the seven-day wake. And in all that time Nontando went about as though in a daze, eyes glazed, and seemed to shrink in physical stature. Her worried sister put the last down to her not eating a morsel all that week.

The family went through motions that seemed well rehearsed. The hired tent was not returned as the end of one wake marked the beginning of another.

Finally, the day that could not be postponed arrived. It was Saturday, exactly one week after Hlumelo's funeral, and Thando and Nontando were burying their only daughter.

And that day, the mother who had not uttered a word since she'd heard of her daughter's death finally broke her silence. Right at her daughter's graveside. And sent all who had heard her muttering and mumbling nerv-ously as they hurriedly crossed themselves.

"God, do you hear me? I don't love you any more. I hate you, God! I hate you!"

Devarakshanam Betty Govinden

Bearing the Stigmata

I sit in the dark pew
abandoned
they shrink from me
fearing the cup we will share
stained with my blood
my diseased black body
despised
quietly condemned
leper of this age

place of condemnation
my Holy Mother
denying me my
birthright
I am
stoned again
for adultery
stoned for my race
for the sins of my brothers and sisters
my cross of shame
uncleanness

You stand in the altar
bruised
head bent
light from the rose window
reflecting the anguish
in your eyes
taking the burden of the stigmata
stigmata in your palms
balm for my spirit
hurt

I hear your words resound through the nave
Those who are whole do not need the physician

You slowly alight
from the cross
and begin
writing with your finger
across the altar
chancel step
altar rails
and down
the
aisle

Joseph Nhlapo

ghost child

within or without
i am all sores
everyday i think is the last,
how can i be sure
am i still your child?

i shout
    shout
        and scream
            for my blood
to spring once again like rivers in summer
nkosi yami! mdali wami
ungishiyelani manje
god! god! why forsake me
am i still your child?

could you shower me
with little raindrops?
could you unwrap
this red ribbon from me?

Antjie Krog
Visit to the Eastern Cape

The sun is already drawing water, but we still have one more visit ahead of us: Canzibe Hospital. We drive and the road is tarred. We drive and then the road turns to gravel. We drive and the road turns to stone. We drive and the road turns to ravine. We struggle across the stones, rev out of the ditches, spin out of the mud and the sun sets over the most beautiful fertile valleys in the country. There is a haze of trees. At the gate the guard stops us. While we wait for permission to enter a young woman in a light blue candlewick gown saunters past with a two-litre bottle of amasi in her hand. She walks through the gate and we see on the back of her gown it says: TB.

We drive into the premises. The hospital consists of a series of small buildings in which separate units are housed. It is overgrown with the most beautiful trees reaching their branches in gigantic stretches of shade across the complex. Lower down are stands of nut and banana trees, pomegranate hedges. But everything testifies to terrible neglect. Some of the large trees have been chopped, or rather torn and hacked, down. Mildewed walls and broken windowpanes. The patients are obviously responsible for washing their own clothes, which lie draped all over the felled leaf-mould tree trunks. Everywhere there are pools of water, rubbish lies around in heaps. In front of the first building is a commemorative stone with an inscription in Afrikaans: *This hospital has been donated by the NG Church Congregation of Robertson. For the love of Christ. 1961.*

Inside the building are four children suffering from kwashiorkor. They sit with their thin legs, skinny arms and unblinking little eyes on their mothers' laps on the floor. They eat pumpkin and pap and there are orange peels on a plate. One woman tells us that she has brought her four-year-old grandchild. She is looking after eight children and her husband. The mines have never paid out his pension. The only food she can provide is mielie meal thinned with water and then boiled. No vegetables, no meat, no beans. Sometimes she does have money for food but lives in too remote a place to get hold of anything other than mielie meal.

There are no sheets on the beds; the maternity ward has a single blanket, no pillows, no towels. And everywhere the smell of sewage and neglect. We are fired up. We demand to see the doctor. We don't care that it is half past six. He is still on duty in the administrative section, we are told. With our list of complaints we walk up the steps, slap-bang into a short Indian man with hair sprouting from his eyebrows and a stethoscope around his neck. In broken English he invites us into his neat office. We look questioningly at one another.

"I am Doctor Kabir and I want to thank you for your noble hearts," he says while looking down at his fidgeting little hands, turning us into the complete arseholes that we are. "We have here a hundred and forty beds for a population of 169 000. We run from here eleven clinics and ten mobile points. The hospital should have five doctors, but I have been alone here for seven years. The past year two Cuban doctors have joined me, which made things a lot easier. We have an X-ray machine, but our anaesthetic machine broke down in 1998, so we can no longer do any operations here. Even caesareans have to be referred to Umtata. We have excellent nursing staff, motivated, hard-working, kind, a good dispensary with all the medicine we need and an assistant pharmacist, but not enough administrative staff. People with the administrative qualifications do not want to live here because it is so isolated."

"Why do you live here? Where did you qualify?" I ask.

"I come from Bangladesh. I worked in western Zambia for some time, then in Mozambique, then here at Canzibe. I . . ." and he gives a half-hearted shrug of his shoulders, "like it here. The area is reasonably crime-free. One or two bullet wounds per month, few stab wounds. Last week some men held up the gate guards with guns and stole two of our six vehicles. We phoned Umtata and they were caught. But the bad roads make the maintenance of vehicles impossibly expensive. We usually only keep half of our fleet running."

"So these limitations do not daunt you?"

"Limitations are relative. This hospital is much better than where I worked in western Zambia. I believe that motivation comes from within and that this is all part of the challenge."

The incidence of malnutrition has gone down, he says. There was a stage when the wards were filled with kwashiorkor children. Personnel are frequently sent into the more remote areas to educate people about healthy nutrition. The women who bring their children to the hospital are also taught about nutrition. Water supply and ways of purifying water have also reduced illnesses. AIDS is a big problem, says Doctor Kabir. It is currently the number one cause of death in most hospitals in the district. In 1995 he did the different tests himself in the laboratory – one in five people were positive then. Now it is almost everyone. "You actually get a fright when someone is HIV negative." The hospital had to have a new wing added two years ago to house all the patients. The poverty in the community makes it impossible for families to look after their relatives.

"Why are there no South African doctors?"

"They don't want to work under these conditions. We had one here from the medical school in Umtata, he lasted eleven days, then he said: This is not my kind of place. Another one in the early nineties stayed for eight months."

We sit there ashamed of ourselves, not even wanting to think about all those who have left the country.

"Shall I take you to the new wing?"

A long passage stretches before us. Doctor Kabir walks ahead. He opens a door and takes us into this lonely place where death has come to stay. From the ten beds in the first ward, stick-thin arms and legs rise. Some dazedly try to lift themselves, others just flutter their fingers on the blue bedspreads, one stretches his arms out to the doctor. One person's mouth is encrusted with sores, another gurgles. The doctor opens the door across the way. Another ten beds. Heat and fever. Another. He continues down the passage, door by door, ward after ward, bed following bed, person after person, skinned into thinness, black skulls with staring unseeing eyes. The edges of their eyes welted with undignified fear.

Doctor Kabir keeps on walking. The helpless, grim anger from the male wards overflows into the female wards, becoming a complete surrender to despair. I see the woman with the two-litre amasi bottle who passed us at the gate. She sits and drinks while tears wash across her cheeks. Out of her frightened eyes still stares the wish to love. Next to her lies a woman displaying almost no sign of skin or flesh. Black bone splint there. No need for tongue. Only breath turning the ill blood over and over. And helpless, despairing eyes. Another turns her enlarged gaze towards me. Not for help, not to blame, but as if remembering herself as a woman, lovely in her bones, living her whole heart's life through days when what she loved was near at hand. Before she came to know only this darkness of flailing flesh, of falling hair. They wait like ferns to die.

This is the end of the world. And I have nothing to make sense.

And nobody and nothing, nowhere, to balm them, every one of them, carefully to lift their limbs and sop them into all that is – my lungs desperately search for a word to breathe from – apple and trellised light. To bathe their blistered tongues in song and cool vowels that fall and fill. To lay them back for the last time on a world fairer than dreams.

147

Doctor Kabir keeps on opening doors. I turn around and walk, and then I am running down the long passage out of these Novilon-clad vaults of misery and dry death. I gasp out into a night transient with dew.

Around me the flowers have grown fangs, but I breathe.

Coldness comes paring down, but I breathe.

Only the moon. The moon showers silver across Canzibe.

And I breathe, in order not to suffocate with shame. I want to blame. I want to pluck someone from somewhere and shake him for answers. What happened to us? Where are all the dreams we once had for ourselves? What happened to our desire to change ourselves, to release ourselves into unsuffering lives, living this land more lovingly? What happened to our dreams to change the heart of rage of this country into one of care? Where are we? Have we forgotten so soon what we wanted to be?

How could we ever become what we would be, if so many parts of what we are die daily into silently stacked-away brooms of bone?

Kaizer Mabhilidi Nyatsumba

Douse the Flames

Once,
    when menacing clouds
    hovered oppressively
    over the horizon
    children braved guns
    and casspirs
    in demand for free air
    and sunshine
    while leaders
    ululated
    and urged them to their death
    pronouncing them
    brave young lions.

Today,
    the fearful clouds have departed
    and sunshine reigns supreme
    with salubrious air truly free
    yet stubbornly
    does a nauseating stench
    hang in the air
    as those to whom
    the future belongs
    perish
    – as if of the black death of old –
    and are weekly interred
    while those who style themselves leaders
    trawl the internet
    deep into the night
    and, with schadenfreude combined with hubris,
    chant nonchalantly:
    a virus
    cannot cause a syndrome.

Oh,
    how we yearn for true leaders
    to douse these flames
    consuming the nation
    to end the wailing
    afflicting our ears.

Dambudzo Marechera

Darkness a Bird of Prey

What are the things, bright-winged
That within me no longer move
No longer 'bruptly leap clear to soar
Towards the stars above this dead-weight night?

Where is that ecstatic turmoil
Which once fired my youth into desperate acts
Visions beyond any known to the hideous devil?
Where! that demented force that hurls Death
"Get thee behind me"?

The hundred knocks on the door
To my thirties-old life
And th'impatient question "Is anyone in there?" – I have
No strength to shudder, to utter, to
Scream YES or painfully mutter "Go Away".

Phaswane Mpe

elegy for the trio

i saw things
as i lay in the blanket
of night
my eyes piercing through the roof
watching twinkling stars
i heard the wind howling
jackals too
& the hooting of owls
the sounds of night
awakened the night of my heart
echoes of thabo manto mokaba
haunted the hall of my skull
drugs drugged
the west tore nkosi apart
& devoured parks
hiv does not cause AIDS
but let thy condom come
anyway
the fear the flame continued
my body blackened
like charred coal
as i lulled myself back into sleep
i heard the echoes scream
my dreams into nightmares
i turned grey & cold like ash
no test tomorrow
i said again

Musa W. Dube

They Should Not See Him

DAY ONE

Yesterday his friends came by. I told them he was on a trip to Tsabong. They stayed for so long, I made tea for them. They finally left an hour later.

Going to that door and opening it was heavy for me, but I did. Chilling shock waves ran down my spine as if I were seeing him for the first time. I shook with fear, not for him. For myself, I trembled. As if to allow me to deal with my fear, he did not move or glance at me. I closed the door slowly. I swallowed a great gulp of air.

"Moratiwa," I called softly. He opened his eyes. They were clear and sharp like stars in a dark midnight sky. Their bright light laboured and journeyed across many light years, past many dark heavens. He looked at me and said nothing.

"Moratiwa," I said again, sitting down beside his bed. "Should I read you a story or a poem or sing you a song?"

I picked up his hand and clasped it in mine. He closed his eyes again. His hand was a featherweight, a bony little structure that lacked warmth.

"Moratiwa, should I read you something?"

He looked at me with a blank face. He did not blink. But I saw and heard the futility of my offer echoed by the thousand particles of air in our bedroom.

"I will get you something warm to drink." Gingerly, I went to the door. Something compelled me to make the least noise possible, to walk with the greatest care, for the slightest sound might be too harsh, too deadly. Everything was so fragile.

Milo, a fortified health drink, seemed the best idea. The matchbox lay close to the dark window. I reached for it, and opened it. All the matchsticks had charred heads. They had given us all their light. It was our last box and it was late in the night. I could not light the gas stove. I could not warm him up with a good health drink. I returned. This time I did not call him. I made no offers and he did not open his eyes. I switched off the lights and darkness engulfed us.

I was up early, preparing Lesedi for school. He was gliding up and down in his soapy bath. "I believe I can fly. I believe I can touch the sky . . ." he hummed a song from one of his favourite movies.

"Lesedi, you'd better get out of the water. The school bus will be here soon."

"The school bus will leave me, Mama?" he echoed my words back.

"Yes, it will, if you do not get out quickly."

"Mama, when is Papa coming back from his trip? I miss him. I don't want to ride the school bus."

Taking a deep breath, I bent down to pick something up, so that my face remained hidden from Lesedi's gaze.

"He will be back. He will be back," I said, walking out of the bathroom.

Soon Lesedi was dressed in his grey trousers and white shirt. He was a handsome boy, tall and dark, just like his father. Lesedi ate his breakfast and drank his Milo. He opened the door to leave, then he turned to me as I sat at the dining-table. I was holding my right cheek in the palm of my hand, like a child without a mother.

"Mama, are you not going to work?"

"I am going, son."

"If you sit on that chair too long you will be late, Mama. You better get going."

"You will be late" – that phrase jolted me with a million bangs. I jumped from my chair. I feared being late. I feared that I was late. Too late.

"Thank you, son. I will get ready, right away," I said, trying to smile away my panic. I noticed that Lesedi was still standing at the door and watching me carefully. The sun was wrapped in clouds that morning, no rays entered our house.

"Are you alright, Mum?"

"Yes. Why?"

"You do not look so bright to me. You look sad, tired or something. Anyway, give me a hug, Mama," he said, opening his arms to me joyously. He ran off as the school bus pulled up beside our yard, hooting. The loud giggles of young boys and girls filled me with yearning for their vitality. Nostalgia seized me. I wished it were Moratiwa and I going to school and laughing happily. The bus drove off. I stood waving until it had long disappeared. "Bye-bye," I said to no one. Perhaps to everyone. I closed the front door slowly. I stood behind the door for some minutes with my eyes closed. Then I walked to my bedroom and I was suddenly seized by fear again, the fear of being too late.

"Moratiwa, Moratiwa," I called. He slept soundlessly. Still. My heart broke free from its ligaments for a second and hammered mercilessly at my ribcage. My eyes were blinded with the great rush of blood, and my hands clenched with fear.

"Moratiwa," I called in a voice that seemed to emerge from a deep and dark hole.

"Moratiwa," I called again in desperation. I dared not move nearer. I loved him dearly. I could not imagine a minute of my life without him.

He must have heard my fear for he opened his eyelids. Once again his eyes shone, making a mockery of the darkness that engulfed our bedroom. Light was life in his eyes buried in the darkness of his dying body.

"I am preparing a warm bath for you. To loosen you up, to liven you up," I said with relief. He was alive. Alive, thank the heavens.

"But first I must help you to the bathroom," I bubbled, trying to shake the fear from my voice.

Gently, I pulled the blankets off his emaciated body. I placed his legs down onto the cold floor. Then I lifted his arm and placed it around my shoulders, while I slipped my arm under his to hold his back.

"Hold on to me," I said. "Hold on tightly. I will support you."

Our journey was long but manageable. Once I'd got him onto the toilet seat, I ran the water in the bathtub and helped him into it. His shrunken body was like a lonely toad swimming in the oceans. I could have counted all his bones with the precision of a mathematician. As I watched him sleeping listlessly in the water, like one who has resigned himself to his fate, my mind was racing for answers. How could I revitalise him? Coffee! The idea came quickly to my mind.

I went to the kitchen and boiled the water.

"Come out, Moratiwa. You have had enough soaking. You are feeling much better now, much more lively. The good coffee will top it all off."

I drained the bathtub, dried him off and walked him to the bedroom. Then I massaged him with olive oil to warm him up and improve his blood circulation. I found one of his expensive Pierre Cardin tracksuits and slipped the soft, warm garment over his body. Then I began to brush his handsome head, gently. I found his Eternity cologne spray, the one I bought for him, and sprayed his shoulders.

When all this was done, I said, "Come, sit on this chair by our glass door. Watch the mountains, while I get your coffee."

We used to spend hours silently watching the mountains of Kgale View. The mountains were an encouraging song of life. They stood there, in rain, in wind, in the harsh sun and in severe drought and still survived.

Even during the night, when it was dark and we could not see the mountains, we knew that they were still there, standing strong. Unshakeable. The mountains were dead and yet so alive. They lived through their death, mocking death.

I walked him from our bed to the chair by the glass door. I pulled the curtain so that Kgale View stood faithfully in front of him. I disappeared into the kitchen to get his coffee. As I walked out, through the passage, I could smell burning. The fire had boiled all the water and burnt my bright little kettle to a pitch-black colour. I could not touch it. What now, I thought to myself, opening the refrigerator. A bottle of fresh milk caught my attention. I got a glass and poured some for him.

He was sitting there on the chair with limp hands.

"Here is some milk, Moratiwa. It will freshen you up."

When he made no effort to pick up the glass, I reached for it and put it to his lips.

"Drink this," I said. "You need food to stay alive. Milk is a whole food."

He did not resist. He drank quietly, like an obedient child. We had been friends for as long as I could remember. We grew up together and played mmantwana together. Moratiwa always played father and I played mother. We went to the same primary and secondary schools. We were even in the same classes. It was only when we completed Form Five that we parted; and then we drifted apart for a number of years. But by then our Thato, our lovechild Lesedi, had already been born. Moratiwa returned to my life when Lesedi was five and said, "Will you forgive me and marry me? I cannot live without you."

It was the happiest day of my life. We were married in less than a year.

"Mama, Mama, guess what? I passed my maths test! I passed! I was the best in the whole class! The best, Mama!" said Lesedi, bursting into the house. He spread his arms to hug me and I folded him in.

"Are you proud of me, Mama? Are you?" he asked, looking straight into my eyes.

"I am the proudest Mama on this whole round earth," I said. I opened my arms wide and drew his joyous body to me.

"You are my beloved son with whom I am well pleased," I said, kissing his forehead. "I want to prepare you the best dinner for passing your maths test. What would you like to eat?"

"Something Fishy, Mama! Something Fishy, that's what I want to eat."

Off we went, with Lesedi jumping up and down like a small happy calf, trotting up, down and across the green pastures. We came back just as it was getting dark. Lights had begun to spring up in most homes except for ours. It had no light.

"Better go straight to the shower, Thato, so you get to bed in time."

"Yes, Mum," he said, radiating infectious joy. "You are the best Mama in the whole world. You know that? You are the best. The best," he repeated, as he always did with everything.

"And that's because you are the best son in the whole world," I said, walking him to the bathroom. Lesedi was in the shower when his father was seized by a fit of coughing. I rushed to the bedroom with a glass of water. It was a cruel sight to watch his skeletal frame wracked by the contractions of the cough. I held him down, and gently patted his back. He calmed down, like the sea after a storm. He slept soundlessly.

"Mama," said Lesedi as soon as he came out of the shower, "is my Daddy back?"

"From the trip? No, he is not."

"I was quite sure that I heard him coughing."

"You probably heard some neighbours," I said, turning away from his face.

It tore my heart that I lied to him. Yet Moratiwa had asked me to protect Lesedi. "Promise me," he had said, "that you will completely shield Lesedi from watching me die and from the talk of neighbours."

We both went over several strategies for keeping Lesedi protected. Since Lesedi spent most of his weekdays at school, and weekends with his aunt, a trip seemed to be the most viable explanation. Lesedi's aunt understood the unspoken and faithfully collected him every Friday.

DAY THREE

Today I woke Moratiwa up, bathed, massaged, dressed and fed him, as I usually do. He did not even want to move his legs. But since his weight is almost nil, I simply carried him to and fro with very little difficulty. It was just after I fed him that I heard a gentle knock at the door.

"Look to the mountains, Moratiwa. Look to the mountains," I said, hurrying to get the door. As I switched on the passage light, the bulb blew. I walked through the darkness and opened another door in front of me.

There in the doorway stood an old lady, whose toothless mouth gave the brightest smile. It was my mother-in-law. I must have been shocked to see her.

"Tlha ga onkamogele?" She asked, jolting me from my freeze.

"Tsena, Mma," I said, inviting her in. In a second, I had prepared all my answers. I knew which questions would come and how I would reply.

"O kae monna yo motona?" She fondly asked as to the whereabouts of her son.

"O ko tripping," I repeated the lie. These days I could say it even without thinking. Like a robot, I was an automated voice that reproduced coded messages.

"Nnare ene o tsamaetsi ruri. Nako tsotlhe fa ke tla fa, o kwa tripping. O bowa leng?" The old woman complained that he had been gone for too long. "Every time I come here, he is on a trip. When will he return?" she asked.

I explained that it was a long trip, since he had gone to audit several government councils in remote villages. I made tea and we sat together in the kitchen.

"Jaanong wena, mma, a ga o bereke go ntseeko?" She wanted to know why I was not at work.

"Ke mo malatsing mma, I am on a short vacation," I told her. In fact, my boss had given me compassionate leave to care for my husband.

She finally left and I breathed a great sigh of relief. I was so tired of lying. But my husband had insisted that his mother, who suffered from hypertension, should also be shielded from this illness she could not cure. What could I do but honour the last requests of a dying man? I watched her walk away, with her old-age limp, until she completely disappeared. Fortunately, whenever she came to town, she stayed with her eldest son.

Turning into my house, I walked through the dark passage to our bedroom. Moratiwa was sitting on the chair with his head hanging carelessly to one side.

"Moratiwa," I called him.

"Moratiwa," I called again, rushing to him. I raised his head and straightened it up. It fell to the other side.

"Moratiwa," I screamed a whisper.

"Look, Moratiwa. Look to the mountains. Look."

People instantly began to arrive. They pulled me away, laid me down and darkened all the light from our windows with ash paste.

Siphiwo Mahala

Mpumi's Assignment

It was a hot Sunday afternoon. Mpumi knelt in front of the coffee table with his books spread all over it. His friends were playing soccer in the open land next to his home and some had gone swimming in the dam. Mpumi's father Vusi was having a drink with his friend Andile in the lounge of the double-storey house. Mpumi couldn't join his friends as long as his father was there, watching him.

"Why don't they go to Andile's place and drink there?" Mpumi said to himself. "They are drinking, and talking, and laughing too. They're happy with what they're doing. Why can't he let me enjoy myself too? I even have to do my homework on Fridays. How can I do homework on a Friday? Doesn't he know that Friday means free? And then there's Sundays. I hate waking up early and going to church. Dad doesn't have to go to church."

The only thing Mpumi enjoyed at church was to hear his mother singing. Reverend Sithole would ask the congregation to start a hymn. Everyone would turn and look in her direction. She would stand up and start singing in her vibrating voice, her arms folded. Then everybody else would stand up and follow. Mpumi felt so proud. He would carefully place his hand on her elbow, conscious not to cover her long and polished nails, which she held deliberately exposed over her folded arms. He would stare at her throat as she sang. Mpumi would sometimes sing, "Thulu, lu, luh-hu-huh . . ." trying to imitate the vibration in her voice.

Mpumi had not gone to church that morning. He had a good reason. He had to do his assignment. He pretended to be writing but did not know where to start. He had to find a topic.

I don't like the school they sent me to. I really hate it. Should I write about not liking the school? No! Only if I want to get zero, he thought.

It was Mpumi's first year in high school. He was often embarrassed by the fact that he went to a school that was previously reserved for white children. Even his friends teased him. They called him "Model C". Boys who went to these more expensive schools were considered softies. No one wanted Mpumi on their side when they played rough games. But now there were no friends, just him and the books and two men drinking beer.

It was at moments like these that Mpumi resented the white school most. The heavy load of homework often stopped him from playing.

His father and Andile were still talking and laughing. They were old friends and were reminiscing about the good old days. They talked about the fights they had won. Mpumi often wondered if his father was ever defeated. Vusi never told a story in which he was a loser, and neither did other adults – it seemed they always won their fights. Just like his teachers: each one of them had been top of their class when they were learners. Vusi and Andile talked about the hardships they had conquered and about the beautiful girls they had admired in their youth.

Mpumi wondered if girls during his father's youth were as beautiful as Nosipho. She lived in Mpumi's neighbourhood with her unemployed mother. Her father was in prison. Nosipho was four years older than Mpumi. She was every man's dream. She looked so good it seemed as if the creator had taken a little extra time moulding her coffee-coloured face. Her small red lips made her look like she was smiling all the time. She had slender legs and small firm breasts, with extra flesh on her hips and bottom. Her dark, short hair was always shiny and carefully combed.

Nosipho was in high school. She used to walk home from school with her boyfriend. This schoolboy had soon been replaced. Another man began driving her home. He was a taxi driver and his Toyota E20 was known for playing all the recent hits so loud that everyone knew from a distance that he was approaching. Most young people liked his taxi because of his fast driving and the music he played. He would hoot and wave to every girl he passed on the way. The passenger seat was reserved exclusively for girls. He would press and pinch their thighs as he changed gears. Young boys liked him too. They used to earn a few cents from him. When they heard his taxi coming, they would know that he was going to need somebody to call Nosipho. The man was Nosipho's lover, even though his belly was really large.

Soon things changed. Another nice car started paying her visits. This new man was really old, the same age as Nosipho's father, but he was very wealthy. He was much bigger than the taxi driver: his braces could not hope to hold his protruding belly. Perhaps he had an assistant to help him put his tummy inside his pants every morning. He was unable to tie his own shoelaces, but he drove a Mercedes-Benz. The man was married with children. Some of them were older than Nosipho.

It was not too long before different cars driven by different men could be seen visiting Nosipho.

159

One Saturday afternoon Mpumi and his friends were playing soccer near her home. There came the taxi driver. Nosipho had just got out of another car. The taxi driver lowered his window, stuck his head out and shouted, "You got her last night. It will be my turn tomorrow."

Other men who were passing on the street laughed. The man who was driving the car also laughed, and Nosipho looked embarrassed. The taxi driver drove away.

Nosipho was no longer quite as beautiful as she used to be. She spent days away from home. She was often at The Ladies Joint, a shebeen where even the wimpiest man got a woman to warm up his bed. Men who drank there were gentlemen too. They never fought over a woman. True socialists, they lived by the principle "What is yours is ours." So they even exchanged women and some men shared the same woman in one night. "If you get one today, don't bother to look for her tomorrow." It was no big deal to get another, just fill the table with beer. The owner of the shebeen had built some flats in the back yard. She let people rent a flat for an hour or two, or even the whole night. The rates varied depending on how many customers wished to occupy the same room at the same time. The prices often increased at the end of the month when people had more money.

"Mpumi!" Vusi called to his son, "what's wrong with you? I've called you twice already."

"I'm concentrating on my assignment, Dad," Mpumi lied.

"C'mon, bring me some cigarettes."

"Alright, Dad."

Mpumi noticed that the soccer match had already started. For a while his mind had been away. He went to his father's bedroom and came back with a packet of cigarettes.

"Thank you, my boy," Vusi said, taking a cigarette from the packet.

He and Andile had the habit of sharing the same cigarette.

Mpumi resumed his original position, pretending to write but actually watching the TV. His father and Andile were talking so loud.

"You mean she is HIV positive?" exclaimed Andile.

"She is suffering from AIDS already. I saw her in Mdantsane last week. I couldn't believe my eyes. She has lost weight and looks very weak. She looks like a woman of about eighty. It's only her skin that prevents us from seeing the colour of her bones."

"No! No, that can't be. Nosipho cannot have AIDS," Andile was saying.

160

"What's done cannot be undone, my friend. Why are you so startled?"

"No, no, eh. I'm just concerned. That lovely girl, still so young to die of AIDS."

Mpumi also could not believe that Nosipho had AIDS. He had heard people talking about HIV and AIDS on the radio and on TV, but he never thought it could come to a person he knew. Andile looked very nervous, like a man watching his own house on fire, unable to put it out. He placed his right hand over his mouth.

Mpumi also became nervous and thought, so Nosipho knows that she will die soon. I wonder how many people she has given the virus to. All those people are going to carry it.

He remembered the day when Andile had called to him as he passed by on his way home from school and asked him to buy him some cigarettes. Mpumi went to the shop and when he came back Andile's kitchen door was open. He could not find anybody in the kitchen or in the sitting room so he decided to knock at the bedroom door. "Yima, wait," Andile had called. Mpumi heard movements and heavy breathing from the bedroom. They were accompanied by a woman's voice, screaming at a low pitch.

After a while the bedroom door opened and Andile appeared half-naked. His eyes were red as if washed with blood, and his body glittered with sweat. He was breathing like a racehorse. His fly was open and the belt was just dangling. Mpumi gave him the cigarettes and change and left the house in a hurry. Just then, Andile's wife arrived. She asked him to open the garage door for her, then called Mpumi into the house with the intention of giving him a tip. At that moment, a girl made a quick exit through the kitchen door.

Mpumi's attention returned to the conversation between Andile and his father.

"Man, remember that earring I used to wear?" Andile was asking.

"How can I forget? I didn't think you were the type to wear such things," Vusi responded.

"Of course I'm not *that* type. You know what happened? When I took leave last year, I often felt lonely when my wife was at work. One day she came back early. Man, she arrived at the wrong time, but I managed to sneak the girl out the kitchen door just before she came in. Later that day my wife found the earring in our bedroom."

"Wow, man! You were in serious trouble. Did she find out who the chick was?" Vusi asked.

"Not really. I got out of it by saying I was trying to be a man of the twenty-first century and wanted to look cool. So I started wearing the earring."

"That was brilliant! How did you think of that?"

"Man, it didn't take too long before I was regretting that statement. That woman made me wear the thing all the time. She would even remind me to put it on every morning after taking a bath. When my leave ended and I had to go back to work it was a disaster. Everyone was puzzled to find the managing director wearing such a thing."

"And that's when you had to stop wearing it?" Vusi was laughing.

"How could I? My woman wouldn't let me get away with it like that. I had to confess to her but I never revealed who the chick was."

"And who was it?"

"Man, you don't wanna know," Andile responded in a very low voice.

"Hey, we've been screwing girls together since high-school days. Remember?"

"That's the worst part," he said with his head bowed and both hands cupping his forehead. He took a brief pause and lifted his head to look at Vusi.

"It was Nosipho."

"What? Which one? The one we were talking about?"

Andile nodded.

Mpumi was no longer watching TV. His attention was completely stolen by the conversation. He watched their mouths as they exchanged words.

"Man, this is terrible," Vusi's mouth was saying. "So, do you think she infected you or what?"

"Anything is possible . . . and I'm worried about my wife. I don't know how to tell her. She's always been faithful to me, and she's warned me several times about my bad ways."

Andile blinked once and tears that had stood poised in his eyes rolled down his face. "Of course, in the past a man achieved greatness by screwing more girls than his fellow men. What we have to realise is that things are different now," he said, shaking his head as he wiped at the tears with the back of his hand.

Mpumi could not believe the change that had taken place right before his eyes. Two men were bragging about screwing girls one moment and a few minutes later they were swallowing their words. Mpumi thought about all he had heard that afternoon. He had seen a man crying. He had found something to write about in his assignment.

Clement Chihota

The Nemesis

Five lightnings crackled around her head
and charged the air with tension.

Her green eyes, glowing like phosphorus,
sent purple points of light piercing
out of the pupils.

Her nostrils when she breathed,
contracted and dilated,
dilated and contracted,
revealing orange insides
that smouldered like fire.

Her red lips, when she spoke
sent flames, more dangerous
than those from a flame-thrower
curling towards the ceiling.

Who was she?
Who else could she be,
but the Nemesis come to face the man
who had sweet-talked all of
his neighbours' wives
and sired in the surroundings
a whole crèche of children.

Vivienne Ndlovu

Lady-killer

(excerpted and adapted from Waste Not Your Tears*)*

The girl beside him stirred in her sleep, and made small moaning sounds, as though she were having troubled dreams. So you might, girl, so you might, he thought wryly to himself. He looked around at the room in which they had spent the night. She had been indifferent in bed like so many of these whores, and he thought with regret of the soft compliant body of Loveness.

Loveness. There was no doubt about her love for him. He knew with absolute certainty that she had never, and now never would, love any man other than him. But she had left him, and at that thought anger crept through his body like small licking flames, creeping from his gut till they finally reached and settled in his loins.

He jabbed his elbow into the girl's ribs, not gently, and she woke with a cry of pain and surprise. Her still sleepy eyes looked into his, and he immediately moved on top of her, ignoring her protests. He was unnecessarily rough but what did it matter. She was only a whore anyway, and he had to still the fire that seemed to rage through him unquenched. Not that Loveness had stilled it. He had been unmoved by her slavish love for him, even irritated by her, but he could not reconcile himself to the fact that she had left him.

Now he was alone, and he knew that his time was running out. He could feel the disease gathering momentum within him. Soon he would need someone to feed him and care for him, and he could not rely on his family. His mother had expected that he, her only son, would provide for her in her old age, but here he was, thirty-seven and dying. Of no more use to her than her daughters.

As he came violently into the body beneath him, he looked down at the girl. She had turned her head towards the door and her face showed only bored resignation as he withdrew from her. The previous night he had been drinking in the Queen's Garden, and the girl had joined him at his table. For once he hadn't been looking for a woman, had been content just to drink himself into a state of stupor while he wallowed in self-pity over Loveness's desertion. But this stupid whore had settled herself beside him and had even been willing to pay for some of the beers.

Zanele, disappointed as so many times before, stared at the wall and watched, as though in a film, the events that had brought her here to this room, this bed, this man.

"Aren't you going to marry me?" she had asked her beloved once more in her schoolgirl innocence when she realised she was pregnant.

"Marry you?" he had scoffed. "I haven't finished my education. I've been accepted at the university. I can't have a wife and child holding me back!" and he had disappeared into the big city, untraceable among the throngs of clever university students to whom she did not even dare speak, leaving her to deal with her outraged parents. Later, she left the child with them – at least they had stood by her – and came to Harare to look for work. But she had no education, and the only job she could find was as a domestic worker.

In that she was lucky. Her first employer was a young couple, with one small child who, despite her fair skin and blue eyes, took the place of the daughter she had left behind. But then they decided to leave Zimbabwe and go down South, and she had bidden them a tearful goodbye. Before they left, they hurriedly put an advert in *The Tribune*. The first person who answered it looked her up and down as though he were buying a horse, asked if she could cook, and said, "She'll do."

After she had been working for him for a few months, she went to make his bed one morning and found him still in it. As she retreated and closed the door again, he called her to come into the room and asked her to fluff up his pillows. As she did so, his hand crept under her skirt. She pulled away from him whispering, "No, baas, no," but he persisted, and holding her still said, "No problem, girl. I'll give you a bit extra in your pay. You're a pretty little thing, you know." And because she didn't want to lose her job, and didn't know what else she could do, she did not resist, and many nights he would call her to the house when her work was done, and send her back to her quarters when the moon was high. It went on like that for a long time. She even grew quite fond of him for he treated her gently. Then one evening he told her to prepare a special meal and when the doorbell rang, a white woman stood there. That night he didn't call her, and when she went to the house the next day she found the woman making coffee.

A few weeks later, the baas called her in and said, "Wish me makorokoto, girl!" He never called her by her name. "Wish me makorokoto. She's going to marry me. That madam you saw," and he danced her around the kitchen. She smiled at him, and then he said, "Of course it's the end of the line for you and me, girl. Can't have you around sharing secrets with the baas now, can we?" He leered at her and took her hand, leading her to the bedroom. "Just one last time, eh? To celebrate." When he was done her gave her her pay and twenty dollars extra, and told her to go that same day.

"But please, baas. Please can't you help me to find another job, baas?"

"I've no time to waste on that, girl. You'll be all right. You're a pretty little thing." He kissed his hand, blowing the kiss at her as he left for work.

But she didn't find another job, and within a few weeks she realised that she had been caught again. The baas had practised withdrawal, and it had always worked. Only when she missed her period did she remember that he had come inside her that last time, remember the wetness.

Once again she returned to her parents' rural home to burden them with another fatherless child. Her mother's eyes filled with sorrow when she saw that her only daughter was pregnant again, but she said nothing. Zanele had weaned Jacob as soon as she could, unable to live with her mother's disappointment, and returned to Harare to look for work; but still she failed to find a job. Now she had two children to feed, one a pale-skinned child who looked quite like the baas. She thought of going to him for help, but she heard he had got married and he wouldn't want her turning up on the doorstep to show his new bride their son.

Then came the evening when she was taken to a bar by a cousin of the family she was staying with. He bought her a beer, and for the first time she understood why it was men liked to drink. It gave her a pleasant floating sensation, and she was filled with confidence. The cousin laughed when she told him she liked it and bought her another. Later, couples began to dance, and the cousin led her to the dance-floor. She danced and enjoyed herself as she hadn't done since she had left school, and when a well-dressed young man offered to buy her a drink she accepted. When the music ended she and the young man were still together but she could see no sign of the cousin. The young man asked her where she stayed.

"Kambuzuma," she said.

"Don't you have anywhere closer?"

"What do you mean?" she asked, by now quite drunk.

"You know, somewhere we can go together. We have to get to know each other better," he said meaningfully. The girl realised that this man had been buying her drinks all night – perhaps he would get nasty if she didn't go along with him and so when he suggested a room in a cheap hotel she agreed. Next morning he left her with twenty dollars. She didn't even ask him for it. He just left it on the cheap dresser as he went out of the door.

The twenty dollars was almost like a gift from heaven. So easy – she thought. As a domestic worker she would have to work a week to earn that sort of money, and without a reference she had little hope of finding another job. She had to earn money somehow and so she said to herself, maybe this way, for a while, until I get myself on my feet. At least I can send my children some money.

That had been six years ago. No more children. She had learned about the pill, but she never did seem to get back on her feet and so there she was, in the Queen's Garden, looking for company, for a sympathetic face. For someone to listen to her story. She was tired of the way of life forced on her by prostitution. She wanted nothing more than to find a man and settle with him to bring up her children. But she no longer believed there were men you could live with, whom you could trust, and still her whole being cried out for the impossible. As a child, she had never imagined any future ahead of her except as some man's wife, the mother of his children, and she had loved her first child's father with all her heart. He had denied her. They had all denied her, yet still she believed what she had been brought up to believe – a woman's place was to look after a man, that without a man she was nothing.

Roderick hadn't expected the prostitute to sleep with him, not without a condom at least, for even to himself now, he looked emaciated, suspect. But it seemed that even the whores didn't believe in the reality of AIDS, and he laughed to himself as he debated whether to tell her she had been well paid for last night's work.

"What's the matter?" the girl asked him. "Why are you laughing?"

"Oh, nothing that would interest you, mukadzi," he replied, pulling on his clothes and throwing a ten-dollar note at her.

Ten minutes later he was on his way to the offices of the AIDS Welfare Centre, whistling to himself, as he thought of the sympathy he would get when he told them about Loveness. Yet while he thought of what he would tell them this time, a small lingering doubt danced under the surface of his thoughts. Being alone. It was the only thing that truly bothered him, and without Loveness he *was* alone, however many people he might be with. He didn't want to be alone, that was what he would tell those white liberals at the AWC. He would weep and tell them he was afraid, and he was lonely. Loveness had deserted him, and he couldn't be alone. Maybe they would find somewhere else he could stay. Doctor Baker was beginning to get on his nerves. The other day when they were talking the doctor had asked about Loveness and Roderick had got the distinct feeling that maybe someone had told him that she wasn't an HIV girl when Roderick brought her to live with him. Although he couldn't allow the thought to surface, it lurked at the back of his mind. What would happen if they found out that he was the one who infected Loveness, that he knew she was a virgin when they got together?

Then his natural optimism surfaced again and he thought: She was a real stupid one. She could have exposed him to everyone, especially that time when she was pregnant with the baby, and he had gone into town looking for a bit of fun. He was bored with her by then, and wanted to get rid of her, but everyone knew they were living together. That had been a mistake, letting her move in, but he had needed someone to cook for him, to feel beside him when he woke up afraid in the long dark nights. And Loveness had always covered for him, even after the baby died. But that had killed the last spark in her, just as in him: it had finally made him understand that he too might really die. But he was Roderick. Invincible. Lady-killer.

In his short life he had had six "wives" including Loveness, although he hadn't actually married any of them, never paid lobola and he had left all of them weeping for him, begging for him to stay. He laughed to himself as he walked down the street. Lady-killer. That was him. Only now it was for real.

Ingrid de Kok

The Head of the Household

is a girl of thirteen
and her children are many.

Left-overs, moulting gulls,
wet unweaned sacks

she carries them under her arms
and on her back

though some must walk beside her
bearing their own bones and mash

when not on the floor
in sickness and distress

rolled up in rows
facing the open stall.

Moon and bone-cold stars
navigational spoor

for ambulance, hearse,
the delivery vans

that will fetch and dispatch
the homeless, motherless

unclean and dead
and a girl of thirteen,

children in her arms,
house balanced on her head.

Johanna Nurse Malobola

Death

who has ever really seen you?
who has ever really spoken to you?
when you come, love finishes itself
when you come, joy stops itself
when you come, pain ends

where are the women working in the white suburbs?
where are our brothers and sisters?
where are the young people of the initiation rites?
death, you are so jealous

when you come, you slink like a cat
your thorn pierces
your hands are stained by grief
death, you are without shame

you harvest where you've never sown
people plough, but you pick
people give birth, but you rob
people heal, but you destroy
until when, when?

every day we bury the dead
how big this grave has become!
oh and you never tire
of the lament of widows
of the tears of suffering
death, you are brave

here are the fat cattle of my father
in the kraals the cows low
the bulls bellow, also the calves
the men laugh happily with each other
but on the other side are tears –
death has come

if only I could stalk you from behind
and pull you down like a lion
if only I could throttle you
if I could jump you into the ground with my feet
then I would teach you a lesson
you, death

Translated from isiNdebele by Bhuti Skhosana and Antjie Krog

Irene Phalula

Kusudzula

It was a chilly Saturday morning. Nabanda had woken early after a restless night. She had buried her husband of eight years two days before, and today there was going to be a kusudzula, where the elders of her husband's clan would "divorce" her and declare her free to remarry or stay single. It was not thoughts about remarrying that occupied her mind this morning because she had already decided to stay single for the rest of her life. Instead she worried about what the elders would decide to do with the property that she and her husband had acquired during their eight years of marriage.

She comforted herself with the thought that since her husband was not a tycoon but a mere clerk in the civil service and therefore had not acquired much in terms of property, his clan would let her inherit all that was left. There isn't much for anyone to grab. Can they really take my household items? Plates, spoons, blankets – really?

As she sat down to a lonely breakfast in her mother-in-law's hut, her thoughts drifted back to eight years before when she and her husband, Wilson, met. Nabanda, just sixteen years old then, found it difficult to resist the tall, muscular man. Wilson had just landed himself a job in the civil service as a clerk in Blantyre. They agreed that she should drop out of school to look after her husband and their future children. Wilson promised Nabanda's parents that he would take care of their daughter. They had a colourful wedding, officiated in a church in their village. A day after the ceremony, Wilson took his young wife to Chilobwe Township in Blantyre.

The first two years of their marriage were blissful. Wilson was a caring and considerate husband, always coming home on time after work and showering his wife with presents even though he didn't have money to throw around. He had time to socialise with his friends drinking beer, but he always made sure that he spent as much time with his wife as possible.

It was now approaching eight o'clock. Nabanda had finished eating her breakfast and she nervously peeped through the hole in the hut's wall that served as a window, to see if her husband's clan had started gathering under the mango tree for the kusudzula. Except for her brother Onani and uncle Maseko, who were sitting on rocks under the tree, nobody else had arrived yet. She decided to wait in the hut. Just as she was sitting down on a stool, her late husband's nephew, a little boy of six years, entered the house and knelt before her.

"Good morning, Auntie. Uncle has told me to let you know that the ceremony will start at ten o'clock," the boy informed her.

"Ooh, thank you, Chimwemwe," Nabanda replied.

She watched the boy walk out of the hut. Immediately she felt an ache deep in her abdomen. It was a familiar pain she had felt so many times in her adult life, ever since she discovered that she could never have children of her own. It was a physical pain as much as an emotional one. Her barrenness left her feeling empty and purposeless.

After two years of marriage and still no sign of pregnancy, Wilson's uncle Ngalaweko had visited them to find out what the problem was. He was a no-nonsense man and very strong. He was said to have single-handedly fought seven robbers who came to the village in the middle of the night to steal his cattle, ripping open the chest of one with his bare hands.

"You are failing to reproduce, Wilson. We have to do something before you bring shame upon the clan. You and your wife must drink this medicine. If it doesn't work in six months I will come again," Ngalaweko said.

The couple drank the concoction for six months but nothing happened. Ngalaweko came back as promised, but this time he demanded to see his nephew alone.

"When a couple is failing to produce children usually the problem lies with the woman because women are the ones who give birth. Nabanda is barren and she is wasting your time and energy. Find a woman to bear children for you. We want grandchildren. Some of us are growing old, do you want the clan to die out because of you?" Ngalaweko asked.

"No, Uncle. It's just that we are not sure who has the problem. Hospitals have not been much help. They told us that physically we are both fine and that in his own time God will bless us. Uncle, I love my wife and I can't leave her simply because she is unable to have children," Wilson replied.

"Wilson, even the Bible says any tree which does not produce fruit should be cut down. When a woman is unable to produce children her husband is free to marry another wife to bear children for him. Polygamy is allowed in our culture, my child. Nobody is asking you to leave your wife. Two years without a child is a long time, people in the village are wondering what is happening and already the clan is becoming a laughing-stock," Ngalaweko advised.

"I will think about it, Uncle," Wilson said.

"Good, you'd better do so or else . . ." He didn't finish his sentence and left for the village.

That day Wilson didn't tell Nabanda everything that had transpired between him and his uncle.

"Nothing much to worry about, Nabanda. The same old story that we have to produce a child."

Nabanda knew her husband too well to be fooled. He was keeping something from her, but what was it?

Nabanda looked at her wristwatch and again peeped through the window. Maseko and Onani had now been joined by two villagers and were chatting to pass the time. Nabanda sat down again.

After Ngalaweko's second visit to their home, Nabanda began noticing changes in her husband. He was now coming home late. At first he would return around nine o'clock, then it was eleven o'clock. His excuse was that he was busy at the office or that he'd been socialising with his friends. Sometimes he would stay away from home all weekend. To keep herself busy, Nabanda started a small business selling fruit and vegetables. She was earning a modest amount which she kept in a bank.

One day Wilson staggered home in the wee hours of the morning and, deciding that enough was enough, Nabanda confronted her husband.

"Where do you think you are coming from at this hour of the morning?"

"From the pub," he answered simply.

"At this hour?"

"Yes."

"You don't look very drunk. Who were you with at the pub?"

"It doesn't matter who I was with. The most important thing is that I am home safely. Now will you shut up? I want to get some sleep."

"You are not sleeping in this house."

"This is not your house. It is my house and I can do as I please."

"What has happened to us, Wilson? We used to be so happy."

"You are very ungrateful. I didn't divorce you even though you are barren. What else do you want me to do? Stay home and help with household chores, hee?"

The words hit her like a hammer. She opened her mouth as if to say something but closed it again without a word. Tears rolled freely down her cheeks and she didn't bother to wipe them. For the first time she felt a sharp pain deep inside her abdomen, a pain which seemed to be coming in ripples, first in her stomach and after a while engulfing her entire body. She felt completely empty. By now her husband was snoring, completely oblivious to what she was going through.

The next day she had woken up early and prepared a warm bath and breakfast for Wilson. She was too upset to eat. Perhaps he didn't mean it. He was just drunk that's all, she consoled herself, he'll apologise when he wakes up.

The apology did come later in the day. But it was more of a confession than an apology. Wilson had had an affair and the woman was pregnant!

"What about me, Wilson?" she screamed. "What about me? What am I going to do?"

"I am not leaving you if that's what you're worried about. I'm taking a second wife, that's all. You are still my wife and you will always be."

Wilson and Edith had their traditional wedding three months before their baby was born. Wilson rented a house for Edith in Mbayani. When Edith delivered a son, Wilson was over the moon and named him Wilson Junior. He took him to his village where Ngalaweko slaughtered a cow to celebrate the birth.

From then on Nabanda's life was hell. Wilson spent all his time with his new wife and child. Until one day he came home to Nabanda with a worried look on his face.

"You look sad. What's wrong?" she asked.

"It's Junior. He's sick," he answered. "He has developed a chest infection. The doctor has recommended that we see a specialist. I need money, Nabanda. Would you lend me some?"

Nabanda was confused. She didn't want to have anything to do with the co-wife and her child. However, she also didn't want Wilson to think that she was jealous of Edith, so she took some money from her savings and gave it to him.

Junior was diagnosed with acute pneumonia and three weeks later he was dead. Wilson was inconsolable. He mourned for his child for months and lost a lot of weight. Edith was also grief-stricken. She too had lost weight and suffered from a persistent dry cough.

"It's stress. She's been through a very traumatic experience. She will be fine," Wilson explained to Nabanda when she told him of the rumours circulating that Edith was showing symptoms of "this same disease".

Months passed but Edith's cough didn't go away. Wilson took her to the government hospital where she was diagnosed with tuberculosis. When she died, Wilson was devastated.

Nabanda was preparing to escort her husband to Edith's village in Balaka for the funeral when her old friend Joyce, who hailed from the same village as Edith, came to advise her not to go.

"Why?" she asked.

"Ooh, so you don't know? People say you are the one who killed Junior and now Edith. They say you are a witch. Her relatives are prepared to skin you alive if you go to Balaka, so please don't go," said Joyce.

"But why? I didn't kill anybody. Edith was sick. The doctors said she had TB."

"Well, they say you created the TB through witchcraft to get rid of Edith and Junior so that you could win back the affection of Wilson. Listen to me, Nabanda. Don't dare go to Balaka."

And so Wilson went with his clan to bury Edith. Led by Ngalaweko, they gossiped all the way from Blantyre to Balaka about what a ruthless witch Nabanda was for not even wanting to attend the co-wife's burial.

Wilson came back from Edith's funeral a broken man. He had lost a lot of weight, which many people attributed to grief. He decided to go to the hospital where he was tested for "this same disease". The results were positive. Despite counselling, Wilson completely lost hope. His legs swelled, he had persistent diarrhoea and had developed growths on his skin, which the doctors diagnosed as Kaposi's sarcoma – a skin cancer. Two months later he was dead.

Chimwemwe walked into Nabanda's hut and knelt before her, "Uncle says you must go now. Everybody is waiting for you outside."

A sizeable group of people had gathered under the mango tree. Some were sitting on rocks while others were sitting on reed mats. Her household items were heaped to the right of the mango tree near the place where the main speaker was sitting. After quickly surveying the group to see who had come for her kusudzula, Nabanda sat down on a reed mat.

Ngalaweko cleared his throat and began to speak, "I welcome you all to this ceremony and I thank you all for coming. Special recognition goes to our village headman who has left other important issues concerning the village to come and witness this ceremony. To cut the story short, we all know that my nephew Wilson passed away a few days ago. We all also know that my nephew left a wife and property. However, my nephew did not leave any offspring. The ceremony today will decide what to do with the wife and the property. When the family sat down to discuss the issue last night we found that there is no one in the family interested in inheriting the widow. The only option left is to divorce her. Anyone with opposing views should state them now."

At this point Ngalaweko paused and looked from right to left. Nobody spoke.

"I take it that we all agree with the decision to divorce her," Ngalaweko said. He then produced a one-kwacha coin and gave it to Nabanda's uncle, Maseko, and said, "With this coin I divorce you. You are free to do with your life as you please. All the people assembled here bear witness to this fact."

Maseko took the coin and put it in his pocket.

"Now let's talk about property. The marital bed, mattress, blankets and bed-sheets will go to Nabanda. I, Ngalaweko, as an uncle of the deceased and as somebody who toiled to send him to school, will get one bed, one mattress and a small radio. The big radio will go to the headman of the village Wilson grew up in."

Maseko's mouth opened as if he wanted to speak. He stood up but was quickly told to sit down. If he had anything to say he was going to have to say it when the ceremony was over.

"The mother of the deceased will get one bed, one mattress, the sofa set and the dining set," Ngalaweko continued. "The younger brothers of the deceased will get all his clothes to share amongst themselves. The sister of the deceased will share with the widow all kitchen utensils. I have already been in contact with the employers of the deceased and his death benefits will be sent to the district commissioner who will distribute them to us. That is how the property is going to be divided. Does anyone have any objections?"

Maseko quickly stood up.

"You can't do this to us. You can't do this to my niece. Stripping her of all her household items. What is she going to do? How is she going to live? You people have no shame. You should have claimed the death benefits alone and not household items, you have no shame at all," he charged.

Ngalaweko stood up again.

"The decision that has been made here is final. Nabanda is lucky that we have given her something. She didn't deserve anything. My nephew was married to her for eight years. What did she contribute to our clan? She came with nothing and she will go with nothing."

At this point everybody was speaking at the top of their voices. Some felt that Nabanda had been done an injustice while others felt that justice had been done. Nabanda bowed her head and was sobbing quietly. She was worried about her uncertain future. Suddenly she felt a hand lifting her to her feet and a voice saying, "Don't worry. Let's go home. I will look after you no matter what." It was her brother, Onani, who had remained silent throughout the ceremony. It was now midday and although the sun was very hot Nabanda, Maseko and Onani decided to leave immediately for their village some twenty-five kilometres away. Nabanda walked away, her empty hands hanging at her sides. She had inherited nothing but her own certain death.

Michael Cope

From the Air

He said that he could see it from the air,
clipped in beneath his glider, almost free
below cloud-base. He said, from there
you spy things that the road-bound never see.
It's marked out like a picture book, he said.
Tucked in away behind some folded hill
the graveyards lie. Here the assembled dead
are ranked by time. The older graves are still
there in their place. Some tended once a year,
some with stones or flowers, dates and names.
The old-time regular deceased lie there.
And all around them, file on file, the graves
of the new dead, packed with red earth
and marked with a cross or a stick or nothing,
and the grass still not grown about them
and the new ones, rows of pits,
and the diggers digging more,
fresh earth in raw heaps,
dark rectangular holes . . .
And round these, fields of clear land, he said,
waiting to be cultivated with the dead.

Roshila Nair

Fanon's land

In honour of the late Gugu Dlamini, Zackie Achmat and other members of the
Treatment Action Campaign, and all AIDS activists in Africa and elsewhere – the
brave people who dare to remind us that freedom is a never-ending journey.

Threadbare in the blood
bloody in the tongue
tongue-tied by the birth push,
we have washed up on a word
like an old bed sheet
wrung dry of the fight
on laundry day

the old world the new world
the new world the old world
(the land! the land!)
if you stared just long enough

love still finds me here
in the post-colonial hour,
here
among the politics of viruses
and neo-liberal economic policies,
here among the grand things
that have curled around us
and sprouted wings
like god's heavenly creatures
vainly trying to transport us to paradise

here in Fanon's no-man's land
we are beginning to learn
how to make everything
out of nothing again.

JJ Eli

Thabo's Tongue

Once, a short while ago, time gave birth to a mighty King. It is reported that the heavens split and the sun turned amber at the moment of his birth.

The people had waited almost three generations for this sign – the indication of the beginning of a new time. Those who witnessed the birth passed the bleeding infant from one to another and marvelled at the swollen Emperor's mark, so clearly visible on the body of the child.

As he grew, the King came to treasure the plains around his home. He adored the mountain, the rugged edges of land dipping into the grey-blue sea. He was raised among people who worshipped the land. The young leader governed well and wisely. He committed to his people in full, and they, in turn, cherished him.

Then time delivered tales of terrible magnitude, spreading north, east, west, south. Like hardy desert weeds the tales blossomed, tentacles of uncertainty and discomfort stretching, on and on just below the soil surface. The King noticed his people stalling, weakened by fear. The entire land was infected. Life and happiness were stolen from the once-busy streets. The people spoke amongst themselves, telling tales of a Beast so violent, an animal so vigorous, that no one was safe.

The King could hardly ignore this state of affairs. He too grew frightened and was anxious to stop the worrying rumours. People from far and wide were brought before him to bear tortured testimony to their encounters with the Beast. Some poor persons were ordered before the royal entourage, the deep scars inflicted by the Beast evident in the display of their naked bodies.

In the final instance the King and his council agreed that everything should be done to beat the Beast. So the King and his advisors worked day and night to educate the people. He travelled, performed, trained and argued. His message became a familiar tune, heard above the songs of sadness and grief that gripped the land.

He taught them not to fear, as there could be no animal, no beast, who had more power than the King himself. And whenever there were rumours of another death, another horrifying attack, he hushed his people and said, "Be quiet, there is no such thing. We have other important matters. No more talk of this. No one can be stronger than the King. The power lies with me."

Sufferers and mourners were shamed into silence. Stories about deaths at the hands of the Beast were repressed. Many cried silently for their land, their dead children, and their lost parents. Each prayed to their god to end the suffering. Pain became private. The people closed their ears to all tales of the Beast. And the streets lit up, lived again, as people loved, fornicated and invested in the future.

But as more and more bodies were carried to the holy places to be buried, the fury of the people grew; firm and strong like eager trees. They hungered for justice in return for the denial of their pain.

Then one morning the King felt a tingling at the back of his throat, making speech somewhat difficult. As the day progressed his taste buds grew larger and his tongue seemed heavy, hanging to the left of his mouth.

Slowly, surely, as the days passed, he became weaker and weaker. He could not eat and mumbled like a fool. At last, all had to admit the horrible truth: the King's tongue was rotting in his mouth. After this he was left mostly on his own as the smell that rose up from his putrid flesh became intolerable. On his throne his skew head bent towards his chest and the pink, swollen, stinking tongue hanging from his mouth.

One morning, as the sun lit the African sky, in desperation and panic, the King stumbled alone into the dense thicket around his fortress.

News of his disappearance sent the people into turmoil. The wise consulted and preached, but to no avail. The King's army was sent out into the forest to search for him and the entire Royal Council knelt and prayed for his safe return.

A group of soldiers found the body of the King in the sand where he had fought for his life the previous night. The Beast had taken particular pride in proving to the King that he was real, punishing the King for denying his superior strength.

It was a fearful sight. The once powerful man must have endured enormous pain. His body was ravaged and his hands extended into the air.

But the worst was his tongue. It had swollen to the size of his arm, green and slimy. It had forced his head back in a macabre position, making it impossible for him to even see the Beast's approach as it attacked.

And not ten steps from the place where he had died, just behind the lush bushes that surrounded him as life was painfully pulled from his body, the troops of the King had lain. Eager to serve, awaiting a sign to defend their King and their people in any way they could.

The wind later whispered to the wise ones among the river people that the King had screamed for hours, acknowledging the Beast and admitting its power. But the soldiers sleeping close by heard nothing, for his swollen tongue obstructed all sound.

It is said that the men had raced away from that horrible place, setting the bush alight in their flight, scorching the land for miles around the King's grave in the hope that the flames would burn away the image in their minds.

They were sure that a new leader would come from among them. They hurried away, agreeing that it would be better to tell no one what they had seen.

Mthuthuzeli Isaac Skosana

When I Rise

Higher and higher I will
Higher above the sky I will
Above the sky
When I rise

The troubles shall remain
The pains shall be healed
When I rise

I shall fly above
Reaching for the sky I will
My wings I shall spread
Yah, I will rise

Behind I shall leave
All the symptoms
All the opportunistic infections
Shall remain
When I rise

I will conquer the infection
I will conquer the syndrome
I will conquer stigma
I will conquer discrimination
When I rise

I will take the podium
I will address the nation
I will defuse fear
When I rise

I will unite families
I will strengthen the weak
When I rise

I shall defeat HIV
I shall defeat AIDS
I shall defeat anger
When I rise
Yes when I rise I shall smile
Oh, when I rise.

Biographical notes

Kay Brown lives and works in Johannesburg, South Africa. She is a property manager and also runs a computer business that specialises in the design of databases. Her two children are now young adults and have left home, leaving her in charge of their father, two dogs and two cats.

Clement Mapfumo Chihota teaches Applied Linguistics at the Zimbabwe Open University in Harare. He is currently reading for a Ph.D. in English at the University of Cape Town. His creative publications include *Before the Next Song*, a collection of poems, and the award-winning *No More Plastic Balls*, a collection of short stories. His short story "The Kiss" is included in *Writing Still – New Stories from Zimbabwe*. He is currently working on another collection of short stories.

Edward Chinhanhu was born in Rusape, Zimbabwe, in 1963. He studied at Marymount Teacher's College, put himself through A-levels and then proceeded to Africa University for a BA degree in education, majoring in English and Religious Studies. He works as a teacher in Mutare, has written extensively for the Education Department and is a columnist with *The Manica Post*. His story "A Christmas Present for Monica" was a runner-up in the 2002 Commonwealth Short Story Competition.

Michael Cope was born in Cape Town, South Africa, in 1952. He has published a novel, *Spiral of Fire*, and a volume of poetry, *Scenes and Visions*, as well as several chapbooks and hand-made books. He has published poetry in little magazines

since 1971. He is married to writer and academic Julia Martin and has three children. He lives in Muizenberg and works as a designer jeweller.

Achmat Dangor was born in Johannesburg, South Africa. A founding member of the cultural group Black Thoughts, he was banned by the apartheid government for six years from 1973. He has published widely as a poet, playwright, short story writer and novelist. His works include *Waiting for Leila, Bulldozer, Majiet, The Z-Town Trilogy, Kafka's Curse* and *Bitter Fruit*. Since stepping down as director of the Nelson Mandela Children's Fund in 2001, Dangor has acted as senior policy advisor at the International AIDS Trust, and is currently the interim manager of the World AIDS Campaign. He is temporarily based in New York.

Ingrid de Kok was born in 1951 and grew up in Stilfontein, a gold-mining town in South Africa. Educated in South Africa and Canada, she works at the Centre for Extra-Mural Studies at the University of Cape Town. She has published three collections of poetry, *Familiar Ground, Transfer* and *Terrestrial Things*. Her work has been translated and published widely in South Africa and other parts of the world.

Angifi Proctor Dladla, also known as Muntu wa Bachaki, was born at Wakkerstroom Old Location, South Africa, in 1950. He is a history and language teacher in Katlehong. He wrote and produced the plays *Mene Tekel, Mistress Magumbo, Dennis the Goat on Trial, Saragorah* and others. For the past few years he has taught writing and produced newspapers with inmates of Boksburg Prison and the youth in Katlehong. He has published a collection of poetry, *The Girl*

Who Then Feared to Sleep & Other Poems, and his poems have appeared in numerous journals and anthologies, including *It All Begins: Poems from Postliberation South Africa*.

Musa W. Dube is a professor of the New Testament at the University of Botswana and HIV/ AIDS theological consultant for the World Council of Churches in Africa. She has published widely, including recent HIV/AIDS-related publications, *HIV/ AIDS and the Curriculum: Methods of Integrating HIV/AIDS in Theological Education* and *Africa Praying: A Handbook of HIV/AIDS Sensitive Sermon Guidelines and Liturgy*.

Mbongisi Dyantyi is a third-year BA student, majoring in Philosophy, at the University of the Witwatersrand, South Africa. He is interested in writing fiction that interrogates African myths and confronts contemporary challenges. His stories "The Runner" and its sequel "The Witch of the Land" (which was produced in the first Caine Prize Workshop and published in *Discovering Home*) centre upon the African afterlife.

JJ Eli is a South African living and working at the foot of Table Mountain in Cape Town. Eli's writing centres around the HIV/AIDS epidemic and related issues in 21st-century Africa. "Thabo's Tongue" is JJ Eli's first story to be published and was a prizewinner in our competition.

 Lesley Emanuel was born in Johannesburg, South Africa, in 1968, and is a freelance editor and aspiring fiction writer. She attends Lionel Abrahams's writing group.

Tracey Farren has been working as a freelance journalist for the past few years, covering developmental and governance issues. While "The Death of a Queen" is a true story, she has also published several

feminist fiction pieces. In 2003 she took a sabbatical from fact and has been working on a novel and a film script. She lives with a husband, pets and two children near Muizenberg, Cape Town, South Africa, on the line between the Flats and white-walled suburbia – a line zig-zagged by roaming dogs and geese, and reckless writers.

Devarakshanam Betty Govinden is a senior lecturer in the School of Educational Studies, University of Durban-Westville, South Africa. She completed her Ph.D. at the University of Natal, Durban and has published in literature, women's writings and narratives, education and feminist theology.

 Khaya Gqibitole was born in 1966 in King William's Town, South Africa and has eight siblings. He attended Griffiths Mxenge College of Education, and in 1994 enrolled at the University of Natal (UNP). He cut his teeth writing radio plays for the Xhosa-language radio station between 1987 and 1997. He is currently completing his Ph.D. at UNP, researching the impact of radio plays on society during the apartheid years. His story "Fresh Scars" was a prizewinner in our writing competition.

Leila Hall was born of a South African father and a French mother in Morija, Lesotho, in 1987. She lived there for the first nine years of her life, and her younger brothers Louis and Alex were also born there. The family moved to England for two years, and then returned to Lesotho in 1998, to Maseru. She now lives in Ladybrand, South Africa, but still attends school at Machabeng College in Maseru. Her story was awarded a prize in our writing competition.

Ashraf Jamal is the author of *Love Themes for The Wilderness*, *A Million Years Ago in the Nineties* and the award-winning collection of stories, *The Shades*. He is also the co-author of *Art South Africa: The Future Present* (David Philip) and author of a monograph on Lien Botha (TaXi Series) and the forthcoming *Predicaments of Culture in South Africa.* He is a senior lecturer in English Literature and Cultural Studies at the University of Stellenbosch, South Africa, and is also an acclaimed playwright.

Nosipho Kota is an award-winning journalist and writer who was born in New Brighton, Port Elizabeth, South Africa, in 1974. She has written poetry, short stories and articles for several newspapers, and her poems have appeared in *Timbila, Tribute, Kotaz, Carapace, Parking Space, New Coin, Community Gazette, New Contrast* and other magazines. She is now working in Port Elizabeth as a journalist for the *Weekend Post,* and is a single mother of a baby boy, Khwezi.

Rustum Kozain was born in Paarl, South Africa, 1966. His poetry has appeared in numerous journals and anthologies, both in South Africa and abroad. He currently teaches in the Department of English at the University of Cape Town.

Antjie Krog has published ten acclaimed volumes of poetry, one short novel, two children's books of verse, and *Country of My Skull,* a work of nonfiction stemming from her reporting on South Africa's Truth and Reconciliation Commission. She writes in Afrikaans and in English. A different version of the piece here entitled "A Visit to the Eastern Cape" was included in her most recent book, *A Change of Tongue.* She lives in Cape Town, South Africa.

Sindiwe Magona has published a two-part autobiography, two volumes of short stories (one of which, *Living, Loving and Lying Awake at Night,* was named one of Africa's 100 best books of the 20th century), and a novel, *Mother to Mother.* She is also an essayist, poet and playwright.

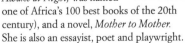

A collection of writing on HIV/AIDS, *It's Up to Me,* and a children's book are forthcoming. She has an honorary doctorate in Humane Letters from Hartwick College, Oneonta, NY. Born in the Transkei and raised in Cape Town, South Africa, she has recently retired from her post in the New York offices of the UN and returned to her home city.

Siphiwo Mahala was born in Grahamstown, South Africa, where he did his schooling. He studied Literature and Creative Writing at Fort Hare and Rhodes universities before completing an MA degree in African Literature at the University of the Witwatersrand. He has had several short stories published in various journals. Two of his stories were selected as some of the best published in the *Southern African Short Story Review* in 2002. He is now based in Pretoria. Siphiwo has been selected to participate in the Caine Prize Workshop of 2004.

Johanna Nurse Malobola was born in Cullinan, Gauteng, South Africa, in 1959. She completed her undergraduate studies at Unisa, where she qualified as a teacher, and has an MA from the University of Pretoria. She is currently writing a Ph.D. dissertation on South African literature. She has published poetry, short story collections and collections of folklore in isiNdebele; her poetry has also been translated into English and Afrikaans. A translation of her poem "Death" appears in Antjie Krog's collection *Met Woorde Soos Met Kerse* as "Die Dood".

Eddie Vulani Maluleke is a student in the Wits School of Arts in Johannesburg, South Africa. She is a spoken-word artist, actress and a writer. "Nobody Ever Said AIDS" is taken from her play *A Woman Like Her,* which premiered at the Grahamstown Festival of Student Drama and went on to enjoy successful seasons in Johannesburg. Her second play, *The Unswept Room*, also about HIV/AIDS, premiered in 2003. She has won awards for her prose writing and is currently contemplating a masters degree and a full-time career as a writer.

 Dambudzo Marechera is widely acknowledged as one of southern Africa's most innovative and important writers. He published, during his lifetime, *The House of Hunger, Black Sunlight* and *Mindblast or the Definitive Buddy. The Black Insider* and his collected poetry, *Cemetery of Mind,* were published posthumously. Marechera was born in Vengere township, Rusape, Rhodesia (now Zimbabwe) in 1952. He studied at the universities of Rhodesia and Oxford and lived in the UK as a writer with no fixed employment or abode until 1982. Returning to Harare, he continued to write until his death from AIDS on 18 August 1987. The poems included in this anthology were written during the last year of his life.

 Felix Mnthali is a Malawian writer who has been professor of English at the University of Botswana since 1982. Before coming to Botswana he taught at Chancellor College, University of Malawi, where he was at one time Provost (Deputy Vice-Chancellor). Besides his many anthologised poems, he has written a novel, *When Sunset Comes to Sapitwa,* and has a number of plays and novels awaiting publication. "Our Diseased World" is part of a longer poem, "Return Jembemziro", a genealogical narrative invoking the author's ancestors.

Puseletso Mompei was born and raised in Gaborone, Botswana. She holds a BA degree in Communications and Political science from the 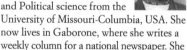 University of Missouri-Columbia, USA. She now lives in Gaborone, where she writes a weekly column for a national newspaper. She

has published several articles in various magazines within Botswana and in the southern African region. She has also worked for Botswana Television (BTV) and is now part of a southern African multi-media health communication initiative.

 Nape 'a Motana was born in 1945. Having practised as a social worker for almost thirty years, he currently works as an advertising copywriter. For over twenty years he has been a cultural activist and founded several cultural forums in Gauteng Province, South Africa. He is a former member of the Gauteng Arts and Culture Council (1996-2003) and was its convenor for literature. He has published poetry in anthologies and literary magazines, including *Staffrider*, and wrote the award-winning play *The Honeymoon is Over*. The Sepedi-language version of "Arise Afrika, Arise!" was performed during a World AIDS Day event in Mamelodi, Pretoria. His short collection of Sepedi proverbs is forthcoming.

 Phaswane Mpe is a writer and doctoral fellow at the Institute for Social and Economic Research, University of the Witwatersrand, South Africa. His first novel, *Welcome To Our Hillbrow*, was shortlisted for the Sunday Times Fiction Award. He has also published articles on South African literature, culture and publishing in a range of journals and books.

Norah Mumba is a writer, social activist and a librarian at the University of Zambia, Lusaka. She has published poetry, radio plays and *A Song* *in the Night: a personal account of widowhood in Zambia*. She co-edited and contributed several stories to *The Heart of a Woman: an anthology of short stories from Zambia*. She won first prize in the Deutsche Welle Radio Drama Competition for Eastern & Southern Africa in 1989.

Roshila Nair was born in 1969 and raised in KwaZulu-Natal, South Africa. She has lived in Cape Town since 1990, where she now works as an editor in the alternative media at a non-profit conflict resolution organisation. She writes poetry and prose.

Vivienne Ndlovu was born Vivienne Kernohan, in Northern Ireland, where she grew up during "the Troubles". Since 1983 she has lived in Zimbabwe, where she met her late husband, Teddie Ndlovu; she writes under her married name. She has published two short novels, *Waste Not Your Tears* (under the pseudonym Violet Kala) and *For Want of a Totem*, and several short stories. For many years she was operations manager for a health insurance company, but has more recently taken up a position as editor and publications officer with a regional NGO. "Lady-killer" is excerpted and adapted from her novel *Waste Not Your Tears*.

Joseph Mphikeleli Nhlapo was born in Alexandra Township, South Africa, in 1971. He studied graphic design at the Johannesburg Art Foundation and DTP at the Southern African Printing College. His short stories have appeared in the *Short Story Review of Southern Africa* (*SSRSA*) and he has had poems published in *SSRSA* the *Timbila Poetry Project* journal and *New Coin*. He also writes articles for the *Sowetan* newspaper. Some of his writing appears under the names Jo Nhlapo and Joe Nhlapo. His poem "ghost child" was awarded a prize in our writing competition.

 Kaizer Mabhilidi Nyatsumba was born in White River in Mpumalanga, South Africa, and later became South Africa's first African editor of a mainstream, non-racial newspaper. He received the Helen Suzman Leadership Award in 1992 and is a well-known political commentator, whose weekly columns on South Africa's political transition have been published as *All Sides of the Story*. He has published five other books, including collections of short stories and poems. He currently lives and works in Johannesburg.

 Irene Phalula was born in Kasungu district in Malawi in 1969. She graduated from Chancellor College, University of Malawi, in 1993 with a Bachelor of Arts in Humanities, majoring in English and Geography. She has worked as a reporter and sub-editor for the print media as well as a senior reporter for the Malawi Broadcasting Corporation. Currently she is employed as a public relations officer for the Sugar Corporation of Malawi. She is married with one child. This is the first time that one of her stories is being published.

Nasabanji E. Phiri was born in Bulawayo, Zimbabwe, in 1980, and currently works for the council in Lupane. "Not At All!" was awarded a prize in our writing competition. This is the first time that her poetry is being published.

Karen Press was born in Cape Town, South Africa, and has worked as a teacher of mathematics and English, and with a range of progressive education projects. Her poetry has been published in several anthologies and journals, as well as in her seven collections, the most recent being *Home*. She has written textbooks and other educational materials, children's stories, a film script and stories for newly literate adults. In 1987 she co-founded the publishing collective Buchu Books. She currently works as a freelance editor and writer, and is an associate of The Writers' Network.

Teboho Raboko's "Sefela" was recorded by 'Makali I.P Mokitimi, Monyane Moktimi and Molefi Mokitimi in 1992. At that time, Raboko was 53 years old and working as an agriculturalist in Ramatseliso, Mafeteng, Lesotho. He had previously been a migrant mine worker in South Africa, hence his use of the oral genre of Lifela, unique to Basotho migrant workers. His complete "Sefela", from which our excerpt has been selected, can be found in 'Makali I.P. Mokitimi's *Lifela tsa Litsamaea-naha poetry: A literary analysis.*

Jenny Robson is a South African living in Botswana and teaching marimbas and steel pans at the local mine school. She has been writing since 1988 and has published several youth novels. In 2003 her novel *Because Pula means Rain* was awarded the UNESCO Prize in the Service of Tolerance. Jenny is married to Matt (who taught her all she knows about PCs) and has two sons, Stof and Doug, who are her inspiration and the lights of her life.

 Paul Schlapobersky was born in Johannesburg, South Africa in 1966, and has lived for extended periods on several continents. He most recently completed a master's degree in Architecture and Urban Design at MIT in the United States, where he is currently working. His thesis, which won the departmental award for architecture and urbanism, focused on the challenges created for Johannesburg by apartheid. Prior to this, he was an architect in Johannesburg, where his practice was responsible for the design of the Yeoville Community Clinic and the head office of the United Cricket Board.

Mthuthuzeli Isaac Skosana was born in 1964 at KwaThema Springs and spent the early part of his life in Payneville, South Africa. He returned to KwaThema in the early 1970s, when families were resettled. He was diagnosed HIV positive in 1996 and began writing poetry after his diagnosis. He is a full-time counsellor and is active in issues affecting people living with HIV/AIDS. His message to people living with HIV/AIDS is: "Don't look down, walk tall and face your enemy." Skosana is married with two sons and a stepdaughter, and has two brothers and a sister. He thanks his family, his friends and colleagues for their support and encouragement.

 Tonye Stuurman is a masters student in the Women and Gender Studies Department at the University of the Western Cape, South Africa. She is a journalist by training and is currently working as such in the Public Affairs and Development Department at Peninsula Technikon. Her road into women and gender studies started in 1995 when she was raped in her home. Since then she has been an activist for the rights of women and children, especially those who have been abused. She is committed to her partner, Dudley, and the joy in their lives is their dog, Misty.

Mbonisi Zikhali was born in 1982, in humble circumstances in Makokoba, Bulawayo, in Zimbabwe. With little to experiment with as a child other than bamboo sticks, old boots and rusted metal, he took to writing. He now lives in Bulawayo, having been a Media Studies student at the University of Namibia. "N.O. C.U.R.E." was awarded a prize in our writing competition, and this is the first time that his poetry is being published.

Nomthandazo Zondo is a South African born in Durban in 1969. She is married and has two young daughters. She teaches grade one and isiZulu at a Durban school. "Baba's Gift" is her first publication.

Acknowledgements

Clement Chihota's "The Nemesis" has been adapted from the version published in *Before the Next Song* (Mambo Press, 1999).

Ingrid de Kok's "Head of the Household" was previously published in *Terrestrial Things* (Kwela/Snailpress, 2002).

A different version of Musa W. Dube's story was published in *Kutlwano* (June 1999) under the title "The Last Three Days".

Ashraf Jamal's "Milk Blue" was previously published in *The Shades* (Brevitas, 2002).

A different version of Antjie Krog's text "A Visit to the Eastern Cape" was published in *A Change of Tongue* (Random House, 2003).

Johanna Nurse Malobola's poem "Death" was first published in isiNdebele under the title "Kufa" in *Itsengo 1,* edited by M.S. Ntuli (Kagiso, 1991).

Dambudzo Marechera's poems "Which One of You Bastards is Death" and "Darkness a Bird of Prey" were first published in *Cemetery of Mind* (Baobab, 1992).

The photograph of Dambudzo Marechera on pg. 188 is reproduced with kind permission of Flora Veit-Wild.

Vivienne Ndlovu's "Lady-killer" has been excerpted and adapted from *Waste Not Your Tears,* published under the name Violet Kala (Baobab, 1994).

Karen Press's "flakes of the light falling" was first published in *New Coin* (December 2002).

Teboho Raboko's "Sefela – Migrant Worker's Poem" has been excerpted from the longer poem which appears in Sesotho and English in 'Makali I.P. Mokitimi's *Lifela tsa Lit-samaea-naha poetry: A literary analysis* (Van Schaik, 1998).

A different version of Jenny Robson and Nomthandazo Zondo's "Baba's Gifts" first appeared in *BBC Focus on Africa* (Jan-March 2003).